Personality

PERSONALITY:

Measurement of Dimensions

by Paul Horst

Jossey-Bass Inc., Publishers
615 Montgomery Street · San Francisco · 1968

PERSONALITY: MEASUREMENT OF DIMENSIONS
by Paul Horst

Jossey-Bass, Inc., Publishers
615 Montgomery Street
San Francisco, California 94111

Library of Congress Catalog Card Number: 68-54939

Printed in the United States of America by York Composition Company, Inc. York, Pennsylvania

FIRST EDITION

68098

THE JOSSEY-BASS BEHAVIORAL SCIENCE SERIES

General Editors

WILLIAM E. HENRY, *University of Chicago*

NEVITT SANFORD, *Stanford University and*

Wright Institute, Berkeley

Preface

I believe that currently available personality measuring instruments are largely obsolete for two reasons. First, the methodological models on which their development is based are themselves inadequate and obsolete, and, second, essential and available computer facilities have not been effectively utilized in their construction. In this book I present what I consider to be the appropriate concepts and methodological models, and the optimal technological and computer procedures, for the development of personality measuring instruments. These procedures are possible largely because of recently developed mathematical methods that greatly augment the volume and speed capabilities of computers for the computations required by optimal measurement models.

The presentation proceeds by four divisions. The first consists of Chapters 1 and 2. Here are discussed the important concepts and principles involved in the development of psychological measuring instruments in general and personality instruments in particular. The second group of chapters, 3, 4, and 5, develops in considerable detail the concept of dimensionality and its relevance and application to the measurement of personality traits. The third group, Chapters 6, 7, and 8, takes up the special psychological, technological and methodological problems and issues that must be adequately considered in the development and construction of effective personality instruments. The last two chapters, 9 and 10, outline and illustrate the procedures for efficient utilization of computers in test construction technology.

I have deliberately avoided participation in the semantic controversies and issues generally classed under the heading of personality theories. These I regard as largely unproductive if not futile. I make no claim to a discovery of what the basic personality dimensions "really" are. My emphasis is on a methodology and technology that will help to "define" objectively rather than to "discover" these dimensions, for I urge that the problem is one of definition and not of discovery.

I have chosen to focus on those methods of personality measurement which utilize pencil and paper type instruments consisting of items to be responded to. I am aware of many of the criticisms of this approach but I believe that other approaches are even more vulnerable.

More specifically, Chapter 1 emphasizes the essential characteristics of psychological measuring instruments such as the stimulus and response elements and the quantification and combination of responses to the latter. The major kinds of instruments—cognitive, achievement, and personality—are discussed as a basis for better understanding the unique requirements of personality instruments. The special relevance of public relations considerations in the development of personality tests is discussed. Those crucial psychometric model concepts that are utilized in later chapters are introduced.

Chapter 2 discusses the particular types of tests which, because of common methodological problems involved, may be classified as personality type tests. It seems important to me to emphasize their basic similarities rather than their superficial differences as others have done. Traditional formats of personality type instruments are presented, and desirable characteristics for yielding good measurement are discussed. Special attention is given to the validity of verbal responses which in my opinion has been unduly criticized. The concepts of reliability are emphasized because of their relevance in the personality test construction technology developed in later chapters.

The extension of the single scale personality test to the multiple scale test is introduced in Chapter 3. I hope that this chapter also adequately exposes the common fallacy of calling a group of items a single scale irrespective of the degree of heterogeneity of the items. The various types of multiple attribute scales are discussed as a basis for a more detailed distinction between attributes and dimensions. The importance of this distinction has not been well understood or recognized in the construction of personality scales. Factor analysis is introduced as a basis for defining and establishing dimensionality as well as for objectively defining a trait taxonomy. It is my opinion that only those who do not understand the techniques and objectives of factor analysis could deny their superiority for such objective definition.

Chapter 4 considers in further detail the types of multiple scales. Of these, I am willing to accord a small role to rational scales but I do not see how a behavioral scientist can give them serious justification. As for criterion scales such as have been developed in considerable profusion, there may be some practical justification but even here I have tried to show that the methodology traditionally employed is not adequately rigorous. Certainly the empirical proliferation of criterion scales violates the principle of scientific parsimony. The use of factor analytic procedures as a basis for generating factor scores is introduced.

Chapter 5 is devoted exclusively to the use of factor analytic techniques in deriving factor scores. I would insist that no other technique has been seriously proposed that can as well provide adequate objective measures of the dimensions of personality. This chapter discusses kinds of factor scores with special emphasis on common factors and computational methods. The item grouping methods are discussed in some detail because their properties seem to have been so little understood by those who have constructed multiple scale personality tests. The least square and integer scoring methods have been understood even less well and I hope that the essential concepts and techniques of these methods have been somewhat clarified in this chapter.

In Chapter 6 I have considered several of the psychological issues that have special relevance for personality measurement. Perhaps the most widely recognized of these is the social desirability variable. I have tried to present this variable as a special case of a more general factor that can occur also in other areas of psychological measurement, and to suggest that its untoward influence in personality measurement may be less than is sometimes feared. I have also suggested how the faking of item responses might be reduced. At a more technical and theoretical level, I have attempted to integrate scaling theory with psychometric theory by relating them to the modalities of the multimode data matrix. This issue seems to me particularly important for personality measurement.

What I regard as among the important technological problems for personality test construction are presented in Chapter 7. Perhaps the most important of these has to do with computer limitations and solutions. These include data and program storage, packing and unpacking procedures, and special techniques such as matrix transposition, obverse factor solutions, and matrix partitioning and supermatrix construction. Methods for determining the number of dimensions are considered in some detail. At the risk of incurring the disapproval of the mathematical statisticians, I do not recommend highly the use of significance tests. I feel strongly that they are not appropriate, for typically they do not adequately take account of sampling of attributes as distinguished from sampling of persons. Of particular relevance is the problem of orthonormal versus oblique transformation. I have preferred the former for obtaining factor scores even though I am willing to concede the superiority of oblique transformations for theoretical and taxonomic purposes.

In Chapter 8 I have recognized some methodological problems, each of which has importance for sophisticated personality techniques. Some of these problems have not yet been adequately resolved for the underlying concepts to have much practical use for measurement procedures, but those who develop personality tests should be aware of their relevance. The multimode data matrix model of Ledyard Tucker is one of the most interesting. The configural analysis concepts and the nonlinear factor analysis techniques of Rodney McDonald are others that will find their way into the technology of the future. The special and general cases of the simplex are also discussed and their implications considered. Finally, the communality controversy is recognized and I have attempted to defend my preference for rejecting the specificity model in personality measurement technology. I have deliberately omitted the nonmetric scaling methods of Guttman, Lingoes, Coombs, Sheppard, Kruskal, and others, primarily because I do not feel they currently provide adequate practical algorithms and techniques for obtaining person scores on the dimensions that they attempt to isolate or define.

In Chapter 9 I have emphasized the importance of the computer in personality measurement technology. Here I consider procedures that might be regarded as the most obvious candidates for arriving at multidimensional factor scores. It seems important to do this and to caution against their limitations, for most if not all of them are already in use. As my recommended procedure I have outlined the method of matrix partitioning and supermatrix construction.

Finally, in Chapter 10 I have presented numerical results from experimental data to illustrate the method of matrix partitioning and supermatrix construction. This method I believe provides the basis for the optimal utilization of computers in the application of factor analysis techniques to the measurement of personality dimensions.

ACKNOWLEDGMENTS

I must acknowledge my great debt to Professor Allen Edwards and his students. Their extensive, exhaustive, and painstaking research with the social desirability variable has influenced my own thinking and efforts in the personality field. If my exposure to this work has led me to conclusions which are not always in accord with theirs, it is no fault of their research methods, interpretations, and exposition. I, of course, assume full responsibility for any differences in viewpoints or conclusions that may remain.

My wife, Muriel, labored long, patiently, and meticulously over the organization and editing of successive drafts of the manuscript. She also must be given major credit for the tedious and exacting task of preparing the index. The preparation of the book and the extensive research on which it is based represent very substantial financial support. For this support I have to thank the National Institutes of Health and the Office of Naval Research. In particular, I wish to acknowledge the continuing support and encouragement of Dr. Glenn L. Bryan of the Office of Naval Research.

PAUL HORST

Seattle, Washington
August 1968

Contents

Contents

Personality

CHAPTER 1

Psychological Scales

*I*t is not the purpose of this book to deal exhaustively with the subject of psychological measurement in general or of personality in particular. Sarason (1966) gives an able and comprehensive account of the history and current status of personality theory, and of attempts to assess personality variables. It is not even our objective to define vigorously the term "personality." Rather, we hope that the discussions which follow will clarify how we use this term.

We may regard personality measurement as a special case of psychological measurement. A great body of theory and technology in the area of psychological measurement has accumulated over the years. This material is available at all levels of sophistication in numerous books and journal articles and we shall not attempt to cite them.

THE ROLE OF THE COMPUTER

One of the great difficulties encountered in efforts to implement the more sophisticated theoretical and methodological developments in the construction and application of psychological and personality measuring instruments is the vast amount of computational labor involved. In this field, as with most technological and scientific endeavors, high speed computers have made possible the solution of problems and the application of methodologies on a scale not previously possible. The use of more advanced models of multi-dimensional psychological and personality measurement has become increasingly feasible, and much progress has been made in the application of computers to psychological measurement problems. However, even with generally available computational facilities, it is to be expected that improvement of models will continue to outrun the expanding computer technology. The speed and capacity of computers will of course continue to increase, but it is still a question whether they will keep pace with the development of more adequate mathematical models and data collection devices.

The most serious limitation of computers has been core storage capacity. The speed of even second generation computers has been reasonably adequate. However, for the types of solutions required by the best available theory, almost unlimited rapid access memory is desirable. It is true, of course, that peripheral storage can greatly increase the capacity of the computers, and as a matter of fact, the supplementary storage available in many large computer installations is adequate for research and measurement enterprises involving large masses of data. But when core storage is extensively supplemented by peripheral storage, a great deal of data transmission between core and peripheral storage may be required. Such transmission is time-consuming unless the transfer rate is very rapid.

It is possible to devise ways to use computer resources with limited immediate access storage so as to approximate reasonably well the results that could be attained by unlimited core storage and more precise mathematical and analytical rationales. The motivation for this book has been the development of a rationale (Horst, 1966a) on the basis of which reasonably adequate approximations to exact solutions for the development of multidimensional scales can be achieved.

This book is based on the premise that the methodologies underlying many psychological measuring instruments are obsolete for two reasons. First, the models on which the methodologies are based are themselves obsolete or inadequate, and second, these methodologies have not most effectively used the computer facilities available and appropriate for the construction of psychometric instruments.

In this chapter we shall review briefly the subject of psychological scales in general and the characteristics of psychological measuring instruments. We shall then indicate briefly kinds of instruments in terms of function or domain measured. Next, we shall examine some of the public relations considerations involved in the use of these instruments. Finally, we shall discuss briefly the subject of psychometric models as a basis for obtaining measurement from traditional types of psychological tests.

CHARACTERISTICS OF INSTRUMENTS

Any instrument, device, methodology, or procedure by means of which we get measures which in some sense may be said to characterize a person psychologically may be called a psychological test. One could, for example, observe a small child in a play school group, note that he is not participating in the activities, and conclude that on a scale of social aggressiveness from 0 to 10 the child has a low rating of, say, 2 for social aggressiveness. We could then say that 2 is the measure of the child's trait of "social aggressiveness." Such procedures are not uncommon in the evaluation of behavior traits. Interviewing procedures in which an interviewer determines the interviewee's rating on some previously labeled personality trait are well known. The interviewer is the measuring instrument and his evaluation is the measure. Such approaches to the evaluation of personality are in use formally or informally in all types of educational, governmental, industrial, and social situations. Many limitations of such procedures are obvious and we shall not here elaborate on them. In this section we shall be concerned with the characteristics of more precise types of psychological instruments. We shall discuss these in terms of the stimulus elements, the response elements, the quantification of responses, and the combination of responses.

STIMULUS ELEMENTS

We shall not be concerned with what goes on inside the individual—his feelings, emotions, thought processes, and other internal unobservable abstract psychological phenomena. We shall not address ourselves to the futile question of what the person is *really* like, what he *really* thinks, how he *really* feels, and so on. We shall rather be concerned with how people respond to various situations in ways which can be observed by other persons, or which can be recorded by appropriate instrumentation. This emphasis implies that there is available an observable stimulus pattern to which the individual reacts with observable responses.

The measuring instrument may be any one of a wide variety of stimulus patterns. It might, for example, be an ink blot, and we might ask the subject to tell us what he sees in it. Some investigators believe that such a stimulus pattern provides a good way of getting at a person's personality traits. They believe he will reveal his innermost self by his unique and specialized reactions to the ink blot. These investigators may have no specific ideas as to precisely what they wish to measure.

Before we attempt any kind of psychological measurement upon an individual we should have some idea of what we want to measure. We may then prepare or provide a clear and unambiguous stimulus situation, such that a person's reactions to it will assist us in assessing him with reference to whatever trait the stimulus situation is designed to evaluate. Having agreed that the stimulus situation is in some way designed to achieve what we have decided in advance that we would like to achieve, let us be more specific about this stimulus situation itself. We might agree that the situation should consist of an integrated and meaningful pattern, such as a picture or some kind of mechanical instrument to be operated or reacted to by the subject, or even that it might be a relatively meaningless pattern such as an ink blot. We shall, however, restrict ourselves to the special case of a stimulus situation consisting of a number of clearly distinct stimulus elements, so structured or arranged that the subject is required to respond to each element of the stimulus situation.

In particular, the elements of the stimulus situation can be test items. More specifically, they can be a series of test items printed in a booklet or on an answer sheet. It is not essential that the stimulus elements consist of words, sentences, or other verbal material. The essential characteristic of the stimulus situation is that it consist of elements that are clearly distinguishable from one another and that can be conveniently arranged in sequence in space or time. The elements can be visual symbols, such as words, phrases, or sentences; or they can be figures of different shapes, colors, sizes, meaning, or content. They may be a series of auditory stimulus elements presented in temporal sequence. Such elements may be of any degree of complexity, but it is important that they be presented separately in time. If an auditory stimulus consists of a number of different tones presented simultaneously, such as a chord, then it should be regarded as a single stimulus element and not as a number of different stimulus elements presented simultaneously.

Meaningful verbal material consisting of a set of discrete stimulus elements can be presented orally instead of visually, but usually it is more convenient to present such materials in the form of a printed test. If the auditory factor is relevant to the particular function or characteristic of the individuals being measured, visual material would not be appropriate.

The stimulus elements may also consist of a series of objects to each of which the individual is required to react in some prespecified manner, as in the case of pegs to be put in a peg board. The elements should not be such that the reaction to one of them necessarily constrains or influences the reactions to other elements of the situation. A failure to recognize this requirement of measurement technology is exemplified by the assembly type test, in which the problem is to reassemble a mechanical object that has been disassembled. From the point of view of measurement technology, this is a poor way to construct a test. It is, however, an easy way; perhaps this is why, in the early days of testing, such instruments as the Stenquist Mechanical Aptitude Tests (1922) were developed.

It may be desired to evaluate the ability to react appropriately to interrelated stimulus elements. In that case a stimulus situation must be defined as a set of interrelated elements to which the appropriate response is one which recognizes these interrelationships. Such types of stimulus patterns imply a highly sophisticated type of measurement, and very little research has been done with them. We shall not go further into this apparent contradiction of the rule that stimulus elements should be independent.

The definition of a stimulus element which we shall use requires that the elements be independent of one another with reference to the responses elicited. Each element is defined so that the subject can respond appropriately to it without having sensed any of the other stimulus elements.

RESPONSE ELEMENTS

For each of a given set of stimulus elements we could request the subject to write down what he thinks is the best or most appropriate response. The results of such instructions, however, can be ambiguous and confusing. Presumably when we measure something we get a number to indicate the measure of the thing we are evaluating. In psychological tests we get scores. If subjects are permitted to formulate their own answers with no restrictions, some method for getting numbers from their reactions has still to be specified. We must, therefore, impose certain constraints on the responses of subjects to the stimulus elements. We shall assume that each element in the stimulus set has associated with it a limited subset of response elements, and that the subject is required to respond in a specified manner to one or more of the elements in each subset. Usually he will respond overtly to only one of the elements.

These elements in the subset are, of course, typically the multiple choice response elements.

Multiple choice response sets may be two-choice, such as *yes-no, plus-minus, true-false,* or they may consist of more than two choices. The five-choice set has come to be used most extensively. The optimal number of choices or response elements to a stimulus item will not be considered at length here. In general, these should be equal in number from one stimulus element to the next. Further restrictions or specifications such response elements should satisfy are given in *Psychological Measurement and Prediction* (Horst, 1966a).

These requirements for a psychological measuring instrument still leave a great deal of latitude for the construction of the instrument. The response elements may consist of a number of choices, one of which presumably is the best or correct answer, as in the case of the conventional multiple choice type item. But a number of variations are possible. For example, the stimulus statement may be phrased in such a way that the set of response elements consists of a series of graded phrases or adjectives such as *never, rarely, usually,* and *always*. Another variation in the subset of response elements provides a series of numbers from, say, 1 to 5. Still another response format, called the graphic rating scale, consists of a calibrated line on which the subject indicates by a check mark his standing with reference to the particular stimulus element. This form of continuous response element pattern is not recommended for psychological measuring instruments.

QUANTIFICATION OF RESPONSES

Let us assume that for each of a series of discrete stimulus elements we have a set of discrete response elements. The examinee may be provided with an answer sheet with a set of spaces for each set of response elements. With IBM answer sheets, the space between the two dotted black lines is filled in with a marking pencil. More recent types of answer sheets consist of sets of small circles; the subject marks within the circle corresponding to the number of the response element which he regards as the correct answer.

Thus the subject does not respond directly to one of the set of alternatives to the multiple choice item, but to spaces on an answer sheet which have a one-to-one correspondence with these alternatives. In the case of personality type tests, the instructions may indicate the meaning of each of the response elements in terms of a series of adjectives, phrases, or a set of successive integers. However, the principle of the discrete set of a limited number of response elements is the same for personality as for other types of multiple choice items.

It is possible, of course, to have other means of responding to a set of response elements, such as depressing a key. For example, the subject can press one of five keys which corresponds to the response element which he regards as the appropriate response to the stimulus element. Here his actual physical response is the same for all stimulus elements.

Whatever the method used to indicate the desired response element, the response is always of some uniform type, such as making a mark or depressing a key. Furthermore, it is an all-or-none response. Either a person does or does not depress a key; either he does or does not make a mark. How gently or vigorously he makes the mark or presses the key is not relevant. Therefore, responses to the response elements may be called binary responses. Such responses are easy to summarize and manipulate with mechanical recording and computing equipment.

The foregoing discussion would appear to set forth rather obvious characteristics of modern psychological tests and measuring devices. But the emphasis on tests yielding binary responses that can be readily assimilated by automatic scoring devices and computing machines has resulted in much criticism. Objections are raised that people are not just a collection of counted responses or data one can throw into a computer. Such objections are, of course, naïve because they fail to take into account the elaborately sophisticated and highly complex considerations which go into the formulation of the set of discrete stimulus elements and the subsets of response elements for each stimulus element.

It should be clear that the responses of the examinee to each of the response elements of each of the stimulus elements can be quantified in one of two ways—0 and 1. If the examinee did not mark a particular response element, this fact is indicated by the integer 0; if he did mark a particular response element, this fact is indicated by the integer 1. We have, therefore, set forth a stimulus situation whose response pattern for any particular individual can be represented by a series of 0's and 1's.

Many kinds of psychological tests and measuring devices do not conform to this pattern. For example, many psychomotor and muscular coordination instruments do not admit of this simplified response pattern. It is probable that much could be gained in the way of improved psychological measurement if many of the tests which have not followed this paradigm in their development were restructured and redesigned to do so.

COMBINATION OF RESPONSES

Let us assume that we have, for a particular psychological measuring instrument and a particular individual, a series or pattern of binary responses. How we get measurement out of such a pattern is the concern of much that follows in this book. A number of possibilities are available. One of these is to assume that there is only one correct response for each stimulus element. If the person has a 1 for that response, then he gets a score of 1 on the item. If he has a 1 for one of the other response elements, he gets a score of 0 on that item. This is the standard procedure in the scoring of true-false or multiple choice tests. The examinee gets a score of either 0 or 1 on each of the response elements in a set for a given stimulus element. But he gets a score of 1 for a stimulus element only if the response element for which he got a score of 1 is the correct response.

We may provide for more finely differentiated responses to the response elements. For example, the examinee might indicate not only which response element he thinks is the best or correct answer but also the relative plausibility of each of the other response alternatives. He might be asked to rate in order of plausibility each of the alternatives to a stimulus element, or he might be asked to assign an integer to each of the response elements to indicate its degree of plausibility. The integers may take values from 0 to 10 or some other conveniently limited range. This procedure may appear to violate the paradigm of the all-or-none response. But we can, for each response element, have a subset of locations on the answer sheet. Then for each response element, the examinee can mark the location which in his opinion corresponds to its degree or rank order of plausibility. In this case, the total number of possible all-or-none responses from the subject to a stimulus element is the product of the number of response elements and the number of integers available for expressing the degree of plausibility. This further extension of response options to a single stimulus element has not been extensively utilized.

Whether the conventional dichotomous or binary type response to a subset of response elements is used, or whether the schema is extended to include a second order subset for each element of a response set, the end result is still a pattern of 0's and 1's. We still need a procedure for summarizing the pattern of binary numbers resulting from the subject's reactions to a dichotomously structured stimulus situation. We have, for each subject taking the test, a pattern of binary numbers in which a number is 1 if the subject chooses the corresponding response element and 0 if he does not. Hence, we have the possibility of a large variety of response patterns for an answer sheet. We must also in some way obtain or develop an ideal answer pattern and determine how the subject's answer pattern agrees with the ideal answer pattern.

In the simplest case, of course, we have a pattern of binary numbers in which 0 would occur for the response element which is not regarded as the correct answer and 1 for the response element which, according to some criterion, is the correct answer. Then the person's score would be the number of response elements for which both his and the ideal answer pattern have scores of 1. This means, of course, that the total score is simply the number correct, according to the predetermined ideal response pattern.

10

Aside from such an ideal binary response pattern, there are other possibilities. For example, it might be decided that some of the correct answers should receive more credit than others. In this case, it would be possible to establish a response pattern of differential weights, either integer or decimal, for each of the keyed or correct answers, and zero weights for the incorrect answers. Then the total score would be the sum of the weights in the ideal pattern corresponding to the response elements having values of 1 in the subject's answer pattern.

A further refinement would be to assign differential weights not only to the correct response elements but also to each of the remaining alternatives in a set, according to their degree of acceptability. In this case, a person's score would be the sum of all the weights corresponding to the response elements he had checked, irrespective of whether the marked response element was the best or correct answer. Very little has been done with such an elaborate procedure of scoring, but in principle there is no reason why with proper validation it might not result in more accurate and useful measurement. As a matter of fact, the general principle of assigning differential weights to the response elements has been used in the procedures developed later in this book.

Not only may one establish a single ideal response pattern according to one of the methods just discussed, but it is also possible to establish several or more different ideal response patterns that may be used to obtain for each person a number of different total scores based on his single response pattern. This principle is also used in later chapters of this book.

KINDS OF INSTRUMENTS

By now our discussion has narrowed to the pencil and paper type of instruments in which the individual reacts to a multiple choice answer sheet. It should be possible to extend this model to other types of measurement such as psychomotor and sensory, and it is probable that such extensions would be fruitful; but we shall not consider them further in this book. We shall, however, as a basis for further discussion, consider briefly several of the major types of pencil and paper tests. For convenience we shall classify them as cognitive, achievement, and personality tests.

COGNITIVE TESTS

We use the term cognitive to refer to the types of tests that have traditionally been called intelligence tests. These may include a wide variety of numerical, spatial, verbal, reasoning, perceptual, and other types of test items. It is not difficult to construct test items, which we have called stimulus elements, together with their multiple choices, which we have called response elements, for these various kinds of content materials. Which of the tests so constructed should be regarded as intelligence tests and which as aptitude tests we need not consider here. The distinction between these two kinds of tests is difficult to draw and may not be worth making. The construction of cognitive or intellectual type test items can readily use the model of the stimulus situation consisting of discrete stimulus elements, each of which has a set of discrete response elements.

It is relatively easy to specify different types of cognitive items. Some items may require spatial visualization. Others may call for simple numerical operations such as addition, subtraction, multiplication, and division. Still others have to do with word meaning, as "same-opposites" or verbal analogies. Other items involve arithmetic reasoning which requires the subject to deduce from the statement of a problem an appropriate set of computations. The different kinds of intellectual abilities for which test items have been developed are limited in number. One could, of course, subdivide some of the types we have mentioned such as, for example, spatial visualization. One may segregate items according to whether they require two-dimensional or three-dimensional spatial visualization. One could subdivide verbal items according to whether they require knowledge of grammar or word meaning or other aspects of verbal behavior. But the number of clearly distinct different kinds of cognitive or intellectual items which one might specify would perhaps not be greater than fifteen or twenty.

12

ACHIEVEMENT TYPE TESTS

There is, however, a classification of items which is somewhat different from the cognitive type and which is important to consider separately because of its implications for psychological measurement. It consists of information type items. In this group are items used to measure progress in school subjects. At the advanced precollege level, such as junior or senior high school, one may encounter a rather wide variety of subject matter areas. In addition to the verbal and numerical areas of achievement of interest in lower elementary grades, there are such areas as social studies, biology, physics, and chemistry. At the college level, one may encounter hundreds of different academic course areas, for each of which tests may be constructed to measure achievement in the area. In industrial, military, and governmental settings, a great variety of information type tests may be encountered which measure the knowledge of examinees in highly specific areas of experience and training. In this broad area of achievement one might specify hundreds or even thousands of specific areas where individual differences might be measured, but for most of these areas where knowledge or factual information is to be assessed, it is not difficult to construct multiple choice items.

Therefore, while the achievement test area presents problems because of the great diversity of subject matter and even though difficulties may be encountered in accurately specifying the areas, the general model yielding the binary response pattern from a set of stimulus elements with subsets of response elements is still applicable. This model can yield a vast amount of useful and discriminating information about large numbers of persons, information which can be rapidly analyzed and summarized by modern computers. The binary response pattern model is equally applicable to cognitive and achievement type test items. The second order subset of choices for each response element is equally applicable to the cognitive and achievement type item. The essential difference between the two is in content and in ease of definition of item type.

The type of item we shall consider mainly in this book is in

13

some important respects different from the cognitive or achievement items. We shall, therefore, discuss it briefly as a separate type of item; we shall take up some of its more detailed characteristics in the next chapter.

PERSONALITY TYPE TESTS

The personality type pencil and paper test has become well known in recent years. We shall not attempt to discuss in detail the meaning of the word "personality" and its uses in connection with psychological tests. We shall be primarily concerned with the type of personality test that involves a pattern of stimulus elements and associated response elements somewhat different from the cognitive and achievement type tests.

Some confusion may arise with respect to tests of social intelligence, sometimes regarded as personality tests, which follow essentially the same model as do tests made up of cognitive and achievement items. In such tests, a situation is presented by the stimulus element, or stem of the test item, involving interpersonal relations of a conflict or problem type, and the examinee is required to respond to a set of response alternatives indicating possible courses of action with respect to the problem situation. This type of item is structurally the same as the cognitive type item, and may be regarded as measuring a type of cognitive ability. It is not the kind of item we are concerned with here.

The personality type test item discussed in this book is a statement about the person whose personality is being evaluated. These statements may cover a very wide range of activities, interests, preferences, behavior tendencies, and so on. One characteristic of the personality item that distinguishes it from the cognitive or achievement item is the fact that it does not typically have a single correct answer.

The response elements of the personality type item have traditionally been restricted to two for each stimulus element. The examinee indicates by marking the one of the two response alternatives that applies to him. It is not necessary to restrict the choices to

14

two; a graded series of responses can be used to express degrees of agreement or applicability.

A personality test in which the subject evaluates himself is sometimes referred to as a self-appraisal inventory. In principle, there is no requirement that a set of personality items be responded to by the person who is being evaluated. For the model we have discussed, it is not relevant whether a person responds to the items as they refer to him or to someone else. As a matter of fact, the latter response reference may have useful applications.

PUBLIC RELATIONS CONSIDERATIONS AND PERSONALITY ITEMS

It is not unusual for psychological testing in schools, particularly with personality tests, to be attacked by parents and lay groups. It is not the purpose of this book to design a grand strategy for combating the forces which attack psychological testing in general and personality testing in particular. However, in the selection or construction of personality items it is well to be aware of the types of items that can elicit unfavorable reactions from influential groups who have it in their power to obstruct the development and application of useful personality instruments. The use of psychological scales has been attacked for a number of reasons. These may involve political, personal, and moral considerations.

POLITICAL CONSIDERATIONS

Attacks on personality tests have been made by politicians, particularly by those with constituents who have taken civil service examinations. It has not been unusual for a person who failed a civil service test to complain to his congressman who then has insisted on seeing a copy of the test and has challenged the validity of individual items in the test. A major objective of testing technicians has been to develop test items that could be defended before congressmen. This concern may be found at federal, state and local levels of civil service organizations.

PERSONAL CONSIDERATIONS

Another criticism of personality tests is that they violate the American tradition of individual liberty and freedom. In particular, personality tests are said to invade personal privacy. For this reason criticism has been encountered among not only extreme right wing groups but also more temperate and progressive components of our society. It is curious that so much emphasis is placed on the invasion of personal privacy by psychological and personality tests without more detailed specification of the disadvantages that might result from having taken the tests. Such criticism seems to be more theoretical and ideological than practical or empirical. It does not clarify explicitly how the welfare of specific individuals may be affected by testing programs.

MORAL CONSIDERATIONS

Perhaps a more sincere, even if unfounded, objection to personality tests is the moral implications of some of the items. Psychiatrists, psychoanalysts, and clinical psychologists well know that socially taboo eliminative and reproductive functions of the human organism become involved in many behavior disorders, in neurotic symptoms, and directly or indirectly in personality manifestations of many kinds. It is not surprising, therefore, that the stimulus elements of many personality scales relate to various aspects of these socially taboo topics. It is not our purpose to explore the rationale or justification of social taboos but merely to point out that they constitute powerful and influential forces within a social system, and that enterprises that become involved directly or indirectly with these taboos invite criticism on moral grounds. This statement should be qualified to exclude such disciplines as religion, law, medicine, and art, which over the centuries have been accorded special privileges, responsibilities, and authority with reference to social taboos.

Aside from the insistence by contemporary culture that certain subjects are immoral per se and should therefore be excluded from personality tests, there is also the attitude that items presented in personality tests may put ideas into the minds of innocent children or even adults, and provide the germs for later antisocial or immoral behavior. Little or no definitive evidence is available to support those who oppose personality tests on moral grounds. Nevertheless, from a practical point of view it is probable that not much of value is to be lost by avoiding the types of items which may prove offensive to large elements of our society; much time, effort, and frustration involved in conflicts with the moralists can thus be avoided. It does not appear profitable for measurement technologists, as such, to dissipate their efforts in attempts to reshape contemporary mores.

PSYCHOMETRIC MODELS

We discussed earlier some of the possibilities for deriving measurement from responses to a set of discrete stimulus elements. We pointed out that typically a good psychometric technique could result in a response pattern from the examinee consisting entirely of 0 and 1 values, and that we should have available one or more ideal response patterns consisting of numbers corresponding to each possible response. In this section we shall consider further aspects of the quantification procedures and relate the rationale of these procedures to modern psychometric models.

SUM OF BINARY SCORES

We have already discussed one method for obtaining a single quantitative value from a set of responses to a psychometric instrument consisting of a set of stimulus elements, each of which has associated with it a set of response elements. The total score for a person on a test can be simply the number of items answered correctly. This definition of a total score implies that there is a correct answer to each item. We may in general assume that whether the items be cognitive, achievement, or personality in type, for some specified criterion or purpose appropriate procedures may be defined for specifying the correct answer to each item. If then a person marks the correct response he gets a score of 1, and if he marks an incorrect response he gets a score of 0. It is obvious therefore that if any psychological instrument of the type we have discussed is administered to a group of individuals, we can construct a score matrix in which the rows represent individuals, the columns represent test items, and each element in the matrix represents the score made by a person on an item. This we have called (Horst, 1966a) a binary data matrix. By summing the rows of such a binary data matrix, we obtain a column vector of scores for the individuals taking the test.

One could also construct an expanded binary matrix by considering as the attribute column vectors of the matrix, not merely the individual stimulus elements, but the individual response elements for each of the stimulus elements. Here then, the total number of variables or columns in the data matrix would be the product of the number of items and the number of responses for each item—assuming that the number of response elements is uniform for all items. The calculation of the test score vector would then imply an ideal response vector of the same order as the width of the data matrix in expanded form. All elements in this ideal vector would be zero except those corresponding to the correct response elements. These would of course be unity. The total score vector would then be the product of the expanded binary data matrix postmultiplied by the expanded ideal binary response vector. This multiplication would simply give the count of the number of correct answers for each individual. These simple matrix operations are presented in *Matrix Algebra for Social Scientists* (Horst, 1963).

ITEM PREFERENCE DISPERSION

One could premultiply the binary data matrix just described by a unit vector and thus obtain a row vector, each of whose elements indicates the number of individuals who responded positively to each of the variables, whether these be merely the correct response elements to each of the stimulus elements or the positive responses to each of the response elements. Obviously, in the first case one obtains a vector of the number of persons who answered each of the items correctly. In the second case one obtains an expanded vector of the number of persons who responded positively to each of the response elements for each of the stimulus elements. Such a vector provides useful information about the difficulty or preference value of each of the response elements. This information is useful in test construction and in the development and analysis of psychometric models. These models are elaborated in *Psychological Measurement and Prediction* (Horst, 1966a).

Presumably, a good psychological or personality scale should consist of items with considerable variation in the dispersion of the difficulty or preference values of the correct answers. The justification for this statement is also presented in detail in *Psychological Measurement and Prediction*. Briefly, if all items in a test are of equal difficulty or preference value, problems are encountered in getting test scores that actually measure individual differences with respect to a single dimension of personality.

ITEM COVARIANCES

If we premultiply the binary data matrix by its transpose, we get a matrix indicating the number of persons who answered positively both responses i and j for all possible values of these indices. This raw covariance matrix, as it is called, may be converted to a deviation covariance matrix or a correlation matrix. Such a matrix indicates the homogeneity of the items, or the probability of responding positively to each pair of items. The item covariance matrix plays a major role in the construction of psychological and personality tests.

WEIGHTED ITEM RESPONSES

In an earlier section we considered not only an ideal response pattern of 0 and 1 values but also a pattern that could have a number of different numerical values for the different items. We also considered a pattern having a different numerical value corresponding to each of the response elements. We indicated that these might be either integer or decimal numbers.

In terms of the binary data matrix just discussed, the ideal response pattern can be represented by a vector of numbers whose order is the width of the data matrix. The total score vector for the persons represented by the data matrix is the product of the data matrix postmultiplied by this vector of differential weights. It is also true that if differential credits are allowed for each of the response elements, then the expanded binary data matrix can be postmultiplied by an expanded ideal vector of weights corresponding to the differential credits to yield a total score vector.

ITEM SCALING

It is surprising but true that traditional scaling theory has not recognized explicitly the primary role it should play in the rational determination of values for ideal scoring vectors with differential weights. Traditional scaling and psychophysical theory have been concerned primarily with the determination of values for stimulus elements, whereas psychometrics has been concerned primarily with the determination of values for persons. The former involves one dimension of the data matrix, while the latter involves the other. We shall have more to say about the relationship between scaling and psychometric theory in subsequent chapters of this book.

CHAPTER 2

Personality Scales

*I*n Chapter 1 we discussed some important properties of psychological scales in general, and we indicated that the personality type scale differs from cognitive and achievement scales with reference to problems of measurement and public relations. In this chapter we shall direct our attention more specifically to the personality type scale and consider various aspects of these scales which are relevant in our later development of multidimensional measurement procedures. First, we shall discuss briefly the various types of personality measures, then we shall take up in turn the subject of formats, the validity of verbal behavior, and the reliability of personality scales.

PERSONALITY TYPE INSTRUMENTS

We indicated earlier that the term "personality" may be applied to a wide variety of human phenomena and that "personality type test" may refer to a variety of psychological measuring instruments. We shall consider briefly various types of instruments that may be conveniently classified into a single group which we shall call personality type tests.

INTEREST TESTS

Perhaps one of the most familiar personality type tests is the interest test, best exemplified by the Strong Vocational Interest Blank (1943). This test consists of a great variety of items that indicate things one might be interested in. Perhaps the chief justification for grouping in one test a collection of stimulus elements, each of which calls for a response as to one's interest in the object or activity specified by the item, is the general agreement that the term "interest" is relatively unambiguous and familiar to the layman. However, attempts to differentiate interest tests sharply from other types of personality tests are probably not worth while.

PREFERENCE TESTS

The oldest inventory using the designation "preference" is the Kuder Preference Record (1939). A later example is the Edwards Personal Preference Schedule (1953). Inventories of this type are characterized not so much by the content of the items as by the format in which they are presented. The content material of the items may be of almost any kind having to do with what a person might say about himself or about someone else. The designation "preference" implies a discrimination rather than an absolute judgment. It is questionable, however, whether this distinction is of such fundamental importance as has been traditionally implied by the psychophysicists. Perhaps all or most judgments are in the last analysis preferential or discriminatory.

BEHAVIORAL TYPE ITEMS

It is sometimes urged that items in the personality type inventory should be statements of specific observable behavior, such as "going to a movie" or "fixing an alarm clock." The assumption is that emphasis on what the person actually does, rather than how he feels or what he likes or prefers or is interested in, results in more accurate measurements of personality dimensions than can be achieved by other types of statements. But this restriction or specification for the item has little relevance for the structural model or the quantification procedures we shall consider in later chapters.

TEMPERAMENT TESTS

The term "temperament test" is of more semantic than scientific or psychological interest. When one examines the items in temperament tests, it is difficult to distinguish this type of measure from others that are concerned with what the subject does or feels or prefers. Perhaps the term has more relevance for various philosophical systems of personality theory than for any scientific rationale or methodological system.

ADJUSTMENT INVENTORIES

A term that has been used freely, particularly by clinical psychologists, is "personal adjustment." As a matter of fact, most relevant activity of human or other organisms consists in making adjustments to their environments. Again it is questionable whether the term "adjustment" carries any implications for item construction that are essentially different from those we have already considered. Commercial instruments, such as the Bell Adjustment Inventory (1938), have perhaps perpetuated an impression of doubtful validity that adjustment refers to a separate and distinct domain of human behavior. The items in so-called adjustment inventories are much the same as items included in other self-report inventories.

ATTITUDE MEASUREMENT

Perhaps the most distinct of the personality type instruments is the attitude measurement inventory. One reason for the prominence of this label is that it is associated with important rational and methodical procedures developed by Thurstone (1929). Thurstone extended the traditional psychophysical techniques to the psychological scaling of stimulus elements. He was not concerned (as were the psychophysicists) with their independently measured physical properties. The attitude statements used by Thurstone and later investigators are stimulus elements to which individuals respond in terms of their own likes, dislikes, interests, feelings, and so on, just as they do to the stimulus elements in other types of personality scales. Usually the attitude inventories are made up of a series of items that refer to some specific entity such as the church or racial groups, or to specific issues, social institutions, or any other subject the investigator can define or specify.

Thurstone was interested in two aspects of attitude measurement. He wished to derive a number for characterizing each item in the scale and a number for characterizing each individual reacting to the items. In other words, he was concerned with both the psychometric and scaling aspects of the stimulus elements. It is surprising that so little recognition has been taken by others of the fact that psychometrics and scaling techniques actually involve closely related operations on the data matrix of experimental observations of a set of entities with respect to a set of attributes.

DESCRIPTIVE RATINGS

An interesting extension of Thurstone's early work on attitudes was its application to the evaluation of one individual by another. One example of such an evaluation has been called the "descriptive rating scale," which consists of a number of different items that describe possible performance of an employee on a job or other activity. Such a scale might be used by a supervisor to evaluate the performance of an employee on his job. The instrument may consist of a number of statements such as, "He is cooperative with his fellow workers"; "He can be depended on to follow through on an assignment"; "He makes few mistakes." Strictly speaking, this device is an attitude questionnaire used by a supervisor to express his attitude toward a subordinate's performance on the job. The response elements for each statement or stimulus element may again take a variety of forms as to number of elements in the set and methods of designation. For example, we may have a two-element response set in which the responses may be *yes-no, true-false,* or *plus-minus.* Or one may have a series of numerals from, say, 1 to 5, one of which the evaluator designates in some appropriate manner to indicate the extent to which the statement applies to the individual being rated.

We see, then, that the descriptive rating form is a particular application of one of the personality type instruments we have considered. Actually, any of these instruments may be responded to by a person as the items apply to him or to any other designated person. From a procedural and methodological point of view it does not matter whether the respondent and the reference individual are the same or different.

Another important feature of the descriptive rating type of personality stimulus element is its implication for the integration of psychometric and scaling techniques. Here, as in the case of attitude scales, one may derive characterizing numbers for each of the persons being evaluated, and also for each of the statements in the stimulus set. The rationale which we shall develop in later chapters integrates the scaling and psychometric approaches so as to yield scale values for both items and persons.

PERSONALITY ITEMS

The preceding discussion leaves little to distinguish items labeled "personality items" from the types we have already considered in this section. Henceforth in this book we shall refer to all the kinds of items we have discussed merely as personality items. The various distinctions that have been suggested refer not so much to differences in the types of stimulus element as to the manner in which they are presented, the use to which they are put, and the way in which responses to the stimulus elements are processed or analyzed.

Our chief concern in the use of the term "personality items" is to distinguish such items or stimulus elements from cognitive and

25

achievement type items. The reason for making this distinction is, as we pointed out earlier, that the response elements present somewhat different problems than those for cognitive and achievement items which typically have a best or unique answer.

Personality, cognitive, and achievement scales are usually pencil and paper instruments. The stimulus elements are traditionally presented on printed forms and responded to by marking spaces on answer sheets. The tests can therefore be administered to large groups of persons at one time—a great advantage so far as administration costs are concerned. But the personality scale has an additional advantage over the cognitive and achievement scales in that the variation in time required for a number of persons to complete the former is usually much less than for the latter. With cognitive instruments it is customary to impose time limits, and in many cases the instruments and administration procedures are so structured that no one is supposed to finish all the items. With personality schedules, on the other hand, it is feasible and customary to allow all persons to finish. The derivation of scores from a data matrix for which all persons have attempted all items is more straightforward than is the case if some have not finished.

FORMATS OF PERSONALITY INSTRUMENTS

It should be clear now that the type of scale considered in this book consists of a pencil and paper test made up of a number of different verbal stimulus elements, each of which is something that one might say about himself or about someone else. We shall now discuss further the physical characteristics of the printed form and the details of the format. We shall consider the statements themselves, the instructions presented to the respondent, the response elements, the forced choice format, and the ipsatization problem.

THE STATEMENT

We have already indicated that the statement may be almost anything that may be said about a person. Preferably, items will refer to aspects of a person that can be reported by him or observed by others, but they may include feelings, emotions, and desires that cannot be observed. About the only physical restriction on the statement is that it shall be relatively brief and simple. A well-established rule for constructing personality items of all types is that they should not be "double-barreled," that is, they should not include two statements such as "I like to go to movies and I get angry when someone insults me." In general, the simpler the statement and the fewer the qualifiers the better. The more complicated the statement, the more opportunity there is for ambiguity and differences in interpretation. A complex statement can usually be broken up into several simpler statements. A statement should be unambiguous unless one of the purposes of the scale is to measure reactions to ambiguous stimulus elements. This, however, is another problem. A practical rule of thumb is that the stimulus element should not take more than one line of printed type; statements requiring more than one line are usually too complex.

On the other hand, the statement can be too short. In the limiting case, the stimulus element can consist of a single word. One method for evaluating personality traits is to present a list of adjectives such as *sincere, energetic, ambitious, versatile, dependable,* and so on. The subject is required to check which of these apply. One of the difficulties in limiting a stimulus element to a single word is that it may not be sufficiently specific and concrete, and may be more difficult to interpret in terms of observable behavior than are more complete statements. It is true that the Strong Vocational Interest Blank (1943) and other inventories include names of objects or subjects. For example, a list of subjects may include English, mathematics, physics, racing, skiing, and so on. To say that such lists should not be included among the stimulus elements of personality scales might seriously restrict the possibilities for measuring some aspects of personality. It is probable, however, that for multidimensional measurement, better results can be obtained with more complete behavioral statements than with single words.

INSTRUCTIONS TO THE RESPONDENT

It is important that clear and unambiguous instructions be

provided to the respondents. These should be printed at the beginning of the inventory or questionnaire, and preferably, in group administration situations, read to the examinees. The instructions will depend on the formats of the statements and their response alternatives.

Usually in instructions to the respondent, it is emphasized that there are no right or wrong answers and that he is to respond to the item as truthfully and accurately as he can. In spite of such instructions, it has been repeatedly demonstrated by Edwards (1957) and others that persons tend to respond in what they regard as the socially approved manner rather than as the item applies to them. For this reason, many attempts have been made to present items in such a way that the behaviors or traits represented by the items are all as nearly equal in social desirability as possible. We shall have more to say about this aspect of personality items in the section on Forced Choice Formats.

Another point usually made in the instructions is that the person shall give his first offhand reaction, rather than linger over the selection of his responses. It is important to emphasize this point for two reasons: first, there is no indication that the results will be materially better or different if the subject is given more time to answer each question, and second, in group administrations if all subjects respond rapidly to all of the items, the variation in time required to complete the questionnaire will be small enough so that all can finish.

RESPONSE ELEMENTS

We have already indicated that the response element sets may take many forms. We shall assume that answer sheets are used with the personality schedule. These may be printed IBM answer sheets, the more compact type such as those developed by Professor E. A. Lindquist at the University of Iowa, or forms that have been duplicated for local use. In any case, the subject responds by marking in the location corresponding to the response elements he has chosen. For each statement or stimulus element, there may be a response set of one or more elements on the answer sheet. Usually there will not be less than two. If there are only two, the subject responds with a mark in one location if he agrees with the statement and another if he does not.

If there is only one location on the answer sheet for each stimulus element, the subject marks it if he agrees and leaves it blank if he does not. Such a format permits the maximum number of statements to be represented on the answer sheet, but this is not an important consideration with the type of answer sheet where many hundreds of statements can be represented on a single sheet. The one-element response location has the serious disadvantage that if no mark is found in it, one is not sure whether it was overlooked by the subject or whether he intended to react negatively to the statement.

For some personality type questionnaires, three response categories are offered, namely, affirmation, doubt, and denial. These can be indicated by *yes, ?, no,* or in any other unambiguous manner. One objection to the question mark category is that its interpretation may not be clear. It can mean that the subject is neutral with respect to the statement, or that he does not know how to interpret it. If one is interested in evaluating the clarity or ambiguity of statements, this objective should be made clear in the instructions and appropriate response elements or categories should be provided. One set of response elements can be provided to express the extent of the examinee's agreement with the statement and another set to express the extent to which the meaning of the statement is clear to him. This approach might yield interesting results, but it has not been extensively investigated. In any case, the use of the question mark category should doubtless be discouraged.

If more than two response locations are provided, it should be made clear in the instructions that they represent degrees of acquiescence or disagreement. As suggested in Chapter 1, there are various ways this can be done. One can provide in the instructions a statement to the effect that in a five-category set, 1 means the lowest order of agreement, 3 means neutrality, and 5 means the highest order of agreement. Or one can provide a set of adjectives ranging from complete agreement to complete disagreement. This latter procedure has the disadvantage that the scaling or assignment of numerical values to the adjectives may not be readily agreed upon. If, however, sets of adjectival response elements are used, the set may be printed after each statement in the inventory. For example, in some scales the response alternatives are *strongly agree, agree, disagree, strongly disagree.* This set of words and phrases may be repeated after each statement so that the subject can mark one of them on the form itself or in the corresponding position on an answer sheet. It may seem a waste of time and space to repeat these choices after each statement, but cost is not a serious concern since, if answer sheets are used, the forms are reusable. It is probable that repetition of adjectival categories on the inventory facilitates responding to the answer sheet location with greater speed and accuracy. In any case, little can be lost by this redundancy.

If graded adjectival response elements are provided, we still have the problem of quantifying responses to them. Sophisticated procedures for scaling such responses are available, some of which have been discussed by Meredith (1964). Simpler procedures are probably adequate. If more than two categories are provided, one may assume that they are equally spaced and assign a sequence of integers to them beginning with 1. One can also use 0 rather than 1 for the lowest number. The use of zero as the lowest point simplifies scoring by effectively reducing the response element set by one category. A disadvantage is that confusion may result because zero may be regarded as absolutely nothing rather than the lowest point on the scale. However, if only verbal response categories are provided, the subject need not know what the corresponding numerical values are.

One must decide how many response alternatives are to be provided. Some experiments have indicated that the more alternatives provided the more reliable will be the results. In any case, perhaps not more than nine or ten categories should be presented. The development of a series of equally spaced verbal categories is difficult if more than this number is used. Perhaps an optimal number is four or five.

One must also decide whether to have an odd or even number of response elements. Ordinarily, if there is an even number, the two middle categories indicate respectively moderate disagreement and moderate agreement. In this case, the examinee has no opportunity to express complete neutrality. If there is an odd number of response categories, the middle one usually indicates neutrality.

In a study by Campbell (1959), the same questionnaire was administered to one group with five alternative response sets and to another with four. As might be expected, in the first case there was a marked tendency for responses to be concentrated at the middle alternative. In the case of the four-response sets, the tendency was for about the same number to respond to the two middle categories and much smaller numbers to the extreme alternatives. In these studies the subject was instructed to respond with reference to how he compared to most people on each of the items. In the five-category set, the alternatives were *much less than most people, less than most people, about the same as most people, more than most people,* and *much more than most people.* In the four-category experiment, the middle category was eliminated. It might be guessed that the results from an analysis of the data would be less definitive with the five-category set where a neutral category was provided than for the case of four categories where discrimination was forced. On the other hand, it might be argued that the more finely calibrated the scale, the more opportunity there would be to reflect discriminations and that therefore the results would be more reliable. As a matter of fact, this latter turned out to be the case.

The most common number of alternatives presented in commercial and other personality type inventories is two. One clear advantage with the two-response set is that one may, according to predetermined criteria, specify which of the two is the keyed answer, and then the score can be simply the number of keyed answers that were marked.

Which end of the response element set is regarded as favorable will depend on the criterion variable under consideration. The direction or polarity of an item can be altered at will. By the use of negatives or antonyms, one can reverse the direction of an item so that *strongly agree* in the new item means the same as *strongly disagree* in the original, and vice versa. The work of Rundquist and Sletto (1936) has indicated that one may do more than reverse the direction of an item by such procedure. For example, "I object when someone crowds ahead of me in line" may be restated as, "It does not bother me to have someone crowd ahead of me in line." Some would argue that the second is not the opposite of the first. One cannot be sure that those persons who responded affirmatively to the first statement would necessarily respond negatively to the second. Very little is known about the extent to which such reversals actually do influence the dimensions of personality being assessed. The work of Jackson and Messick (1958) on response styles throws some light on this question, but perhaps more sophisticated mathematical models than those they employed are required to yield definitive results.

FORCED CHOICE FORMATS

The tendency of persons to give socially desirable responses to personality type items rather than the responses which actually apply has already been mentioned. The work of Edwards (1957) and his students gives ample verification of this tendency. The problem of how to get persons to give responses that apply to themselves rather than to their concept of the ideal person has motivated a great deal of research effort. In the simplest type of personality questionnaire it has been customary to list the items in random sequence. The tendency then is to agree with the items that suggest socially desirable behavior and to disagree with those indicating undesirable behavior.

By means of traditional scaling techniques, it is possible to assign social desirability scale values to the items on the basis of results from an experimental group. Many studies indicate that almost any method of scaling the items gives scale values which correlate highly with the endorsement percentages obtained by administering the questionnaire to some other group. This relationship has been found to be relatively constant for a wide variety of items, and for many different groups varying in nationality, economic level, education, sex, and so on. The character of the group used for scaling the items and the group being tested by the instrument appears to make little difference.

A procedure used to overcome this difficulty begins by segregating items according to their scale values. Pairs of items are then chosen so that both have about the same social desirability value but are assumed to measure different traits. Such pairs of items are then presented in the questionnaire format in pairs. For each pair the subject is required to indicate which one of the pair best describes him. Presumably then, the choice is made not on the basis of the most socially desirable item but rather on the basis of the trait the subject regards himself as having the most of. In this procedure it is necessary to start with some set of postulated traits. The total number of items from each trait is about equal in the entire set of pairs. A person's score for each trait is the number of times that an item from that trait set was preferred by the examinee. With this format a stimulus element consists of a pair of items and the response set consists of two elements. A response to one of the two response elements means a person prefers the corresponding statement in the stimulus element.

It is not necessary that the number of items in the forced choice format be restricted to two items. The Kuder Preference Record (1939) and other schedules have used more than two items in a stimulus element. It is possible to present sets of items for each of which the subject expresses his rank order preference for the members of the set. For sets of three items, he may be asked to indicate the one that best describes him and the one that least describes him.

In any case, with the forced choice format it is important that the items be grouped according to some predesigned system which hypothesizes a set of traits or dimensions. It is also important that the design or pattern of item grouping be accompanied with scoring procedures that may logically yield measures of the traits hypothesized.

IPSATIZATION PROBLEM IN FORCED CHOICE FORMAT

One problem encountered in the forced choice format,

whether the groups consist of two or more than two items, is that the particular groupings of items and scoring procedures result in the loss of important information. If a person says that one item describes him better than the other or that he prefers one thing to another, this tells nothing about how he rates himself on these items relative to other persons. Therefore the forced choice formats yield only intra-individual evaluations rather than inter-individual evaluations.

Also, a scale involving the forced choice format cannot be a unidimensional scale. The use of the forced choice format requires that the instrument yield a number of different scales and that the responses which subjects make are based on discriminations between stimulus elements from two or more different scales. If the instrument is designed to measure only a single trait or dimension, the forced choice procedure is not applicable. It is important to recognize this limitation of the procedure. The properties and limitations of ipsatized variables in general have been discussed by Clemans (1966).

VALIDITY OF VERBAL RESPONSES

The preceding discussions may imply that the ideal way to measure personality dimensions is by means of ones responses to verbal statements about themselves. Certainly human beings react in many socially significant ways other than those typified by responses to personality questionnaires. There has been much criticism of the use of pencil and paper tests for measuring personality dimensions. Many have insisted that the information obtained from personality questionnaires does not really measure personality and that human beings are far too complex to be evaluated even approximately by such narrowly specialized instruments as personality tests. In spite of these doubts and the obvious limitations of the personality questionnaire, it is still possible that much of the socially significant behavior of human organisms can be assessed directly or indirectly by means of these tests. One may also question to what extent those aspects of human personality that cannot be so evaluated can be evaluated with demonstrated accuracy by other means.

We shall examine briefly some of the issues relating to validity and adequacy of personality measurement by means of responses to verbal stimuli. We shall consider the temporal stability of responses to verbal material, the adequacies of self-appraisals, the possibilities and limitations of external appraisers, the subjective nature of right-answer specifications, uniqueness of verbal behavior to man, and the problem of false responses to items.

TEMPORAL STABILITY OF RESPONSES TO VERBAL MATERIAL

By administering a stimulus set to the same group of individuals repeatedly, it is possible to determine the stability of responses to these stimulus elements over time. A person's responses to personality items can change over time in two ways: a systematic shift may be noted, or random variations may occur. We may have a personality item such as "Republicans are too conservative," to which a young man may respond with strong agreement. Over time as he progresses in a large industrial organization from one rung of the ladder to a higher one, he may gradually change from agreement to disagreement. On the other hand, the attitude of another youth may fluctuate. At times he may think that Republicans are too conservative, at other times, after listening to an eloquent Republican campaigner, he may decide that Republicans are not too conservative. It is this latter kind of change which primarily concerns us when we consider the temporal stability of verbal responses. Actually, however, we are not so much concerned with the stability of a person's responses to a single item. If responses from enough items are obtained, the stability of a total score may be adequate even though responses to individual items may fluctuate considerably over a period of time.

VALIDITY OF SELF-APPRAISALS

One criticism of the personality type inventory is that what the person says about himself may not be true. Even if he tries to be as honest and accurate as possible, it is asserted that a person may not know himself sufficiently well to give accurate responses to the inventory items. A person who says that "Republicans are too conservative" may really not believe this to be the case; he may agree with most of the things that Republicans stand for. A person may say that he objects strenuously whenever someone crowds ahead of him in a line, but observers who have seen people crowding ahead of him may report that he does not object strenuously, and will therefore insist that his response is not valid. There may, of course, be great variation in the extent to which people, even if they wish to be truthful, can give accurate responses to statements about themselves.

However, again we are not so much concerned with the reactions of persons to individual items. The validity of responses to individual items is not so important when considered in the broader methodological context we shall develop later. What interests us more are the characteristics of measures which we derive from these responses. These characteristics will be discussed in later chapters.

VALIDITY OF THE EXTERNAL APPRAISER

Earlier in this chapter we discussed the descriptive rating scale in which a person marks the answer sheet according to the way it applies to some other individual. We may well ask whether a supervisor is sufficiently familiar with all aspects of an employee's performance on the job that he can respond accurately and validly to each stimulus element in the appraisal instrument. But, as in the case of self-appraisal, we are not so much concerned with the question of whether the supervisor "really" knows which response elements should be checked for a given employee as we are in certain statistical characteristics of a data matrix obtained by external appraisers on a number of individuals. We shall consider these characteristics in detail in later chapters. It is enough to point out here that the question of the validity of the external appraiser, like that of the validity of the responses to stimuli in general, cannot be settled by purely rational discussions and a priori judgments.

SUBJECTIVITY OF THE BEST ANSWER

In general, a personality item does not have one right answer as does a cognitive or an achievement item. The right answer for a cognitive or an achievement item is usually assumed to be the same for every one. For personality items the phrase "right answer" has meaning only in terms of some specified definition of "rightness." The right answer for one person may not be the right answer for another.

In cognitive and achievement tests the item itself is the stimulus element, whereas in the personality test the stimulus element is the combination of the item and the person responding to it. The person himself is part of the situation being reacted to. The role of the participant in the stimulus element largely distinguishes the personality scale from other scales. The inventory is a distinct and separate inventory for each person who responds to it. This way of looking at the model is more than an exercise in verbal gymnastics, as we shall see later.

VALIDITY OF VERBAL BEHAVIOR

One objection to the use of verbal material for evaluating personality dimensions is that such stimuli evoke only a limited sampling of all of the responses that characterize one's personality. Verbal stimulus situations constitute only a part of a wide variety of stimulus complexes to which human beings respond in ways which differentiate them from one another with respect to socially important variables. On the other hand, it is probable that the significance and importance of responses to verbal stimulus situations have been underestimated. One important difference between man and other higher vertebrates is the elaborate communication systems man has developed and the fundamental role of these systems in his adjustment to his social environment.

Perhaps the most mysterious part of the human organism is the brain. Many of its manifestations occur in the form of communication symbols such as spoken or written words, chemical formulas, mathematical equations, musical scores, dance notation, or blueprints. These symbolic systems generated by the brain can be translated into patterns of oral or written verbal symbols, even though these verbal patterns are not necessarily the most efficient. Nevertheless, it is probable that most of the behavior dimensions of interest to human beings in a collective society and those which distinguish them from the lower vertebrates can find their correspondences in verbal patterns.

Psychologists have perhaps been unduly diffident in the use of verbal statements for the assessment of personality dimensions. It is also probable that the critics of this approach have unduly exaggerated the importance of those aspects of human behavior that cannot be assessed directly or indirectly through the use of verbal stimulus elements.

RELEVANCE OF FAKING

We have already mentioned the criticisms of those who question the validity of verbal responses because of the inability or unwillingness of persons to react accurately and appropriately to individual items. We have discussed the tendency for persons to give responses that are thought to be socially desirable rather than the responses that apply to them. Obviously, such reactions do not conform to the model which regards a stimulus element as the combination of the statement and the person responding. People who respond in the socially desirable manner are treating a personality item as though it were a cognitive or achievement item. They imply that there is a best answer. We are not concerned here with questions of morality and truthfulness but rather with a basic difference in paradigms which distinguishes achievement and cognitive items from personality items. One of the problems in the measurement of personality by means of verbal stimulus elements is the structuring of the situations so that the respondent becomes an integral part of those situations.

RELIABILITY OF PERSONALITY SCALES

Earlier in this chapter we discussed one type of test reliability as traditionally treated in textbooks on psychological measurement theory. In *Psychological Measurement and Prediction* (Horst, 1966a) the traditional concepts of reliability, together with criticisms and suggestions for modification of these concepts, are presented. Since the concepts usually included under the heading of reliability are of considerable technical importance for the development of personality scales, we shall give some attention to them in this section. The discussion will not attempt to be exhaustive but should provide adequate background for the technological, methodological, and procedural topics to be discussed in later chapters. We shall consider three types of reliability usually presented in discussions of the subject—comparable form reliability, homogeneity as an estimate of reliability, and retest reliability.

COMPARABLE FORM RELIABILITY

One method of determining the reliability of a test uses two or more test forms that purport to measure the same function. Two of these comparable forms are administered to the same group of persons and the two sets of scores are then correlated. The correlation between the two sets of scores is often called the reliability of the test.

It has been common practice in test construction enterprises to prepare a number of test forms for a given test. Often the specifications of what the test measures have been vague and unsatisfactory. Nevertheless, in practical situations it has been possible to develop, for example, two forms of a test to measure arithmetic ability at the fifth grade level, or to make several forms of an aptitude test as the College Board does each year with its Scholastic Aptitude Examination. This latter examination is not a test of a single dimension but a composite of different kinds of items assembled from a large pool of items into a single instrument. Other instruments similarly assembled from this pool of items are assumed to provide measures comparable to the original instrument and to each other.

It is important to recognize that the construction of a number of different forms presumed to measure the same things implies rigorous models, specifications, and experimental procedures to assure that the forms are in fact measuring the same things. The criteria for determining whether forms are comparable are discussed in some detail in *Psychological Measurement and Prediction* (Horst, 1966a).

The concept of comparable form reliability has not been generally used in connection with personality inventories designed to yield multiple sets of scores. Traditional personality instruments are now in use which purport to yield scores on a number of different scales, sometimes as many as forty.

Comparable form reliability has been based on a model that assumes a universe of items within a given domain and the sampling of items from this universe. Such a model is probably too naïve and too much restricted by the traditional assumptions of the mathematical statistician. It does not appear to meet the requirements of an adequately sophisticated measurement technology. This point we shall develop further when we discuss the role of factor analysis in psychological measurement.

TEST HOMOGENEITY

We have mentioned the item covariance matrix which involves calculating the minor product moment of the data matrix. This matrix gives the number of persons who respond jointly to all possible pairs of response elements in the inventory. In right-answer type tests, covariance matrices show to what extent any two items measure the same function. If all who answer one item correctly also answer another correctly, we may assume that one of the items provides the same information as the two together. Items are said to be perfectly homogeneous within a set if all persons who answer correctly a more difficult item also answer correctly less difficult items. In actual practice, of course, one never encounters this ideal situation.

One could theoretically construct a number of sets of items which are homogeneous within sets but are heterogeneous between sets. Then by definition the scores made on one test would be uncorrelated with those made on another. The distinction between intra-test and inter-test item homogeneity is important whenever homogeneity is used to estimate test reliability.

Measures of intra-test item homogeneity have often been used to estimate test reliability. Procedures were developed for this purpose by Kuder and Richardson (1937) and have led to the well-known Kuder-Richardson formula 21. This formula has proved useful, but unfortunately it has also been misused. Homogeneity estimates, as we have shown in *Psychological Measurement and Prediction* (Horst, 1966a), can be used as a basis for estimating the *limits* of test reliability, but they are not strictly speaking measures of reliability.

In any case, homogeneity estimates of reliability have been used frequently for personality scales. Personality instruments have been developed to yield multidimensional scales by segregating subsets of items which purport to measure unique dimensions. This approach has serious limitations, but it also has advantages in that simplified scoring procedures are possible. If the scales derived from a single instrument are based on segregated groups of items, then for each subgroup one can apply the Kuder-Richardson formula or other appropriate index of homogeneity to obtain a rough estimate of the reliability of the scale. Advantages of the Kuder-Richardson or similar homogeneity indices for estimating reliability are the ease with which they can be calculated, and the fact that alternate or comparable forms are not required.

RETEST RELIABILITY

Perhaps the most useful concept subsumed under the title of test reliability is that of temporal stability. If we take a measurement of an individual at one time, how sure can we be that this represents his performance at another time, assuming that he does not change systematically with age or experience? How accurately can we predict a person's responses from one administration of a psychological measuring instrument to another administration a week or two weeks later? Retest reliability is probably the most realistic and useful concept of test reliability from both a practical and theoretical point of view. In later chapters we shall show how the concept of retest reliability appears as a special case of the three-mode data matrix developed by Tucker (1963) which includes, in addition to the traditional modes of entities and attributes, also the occasion mode.

CHAPTER 3

Dimensions in Personality Measurement

*P*erhaps one of the most important concepts in science is that of dimensionality, a concept that has been discussed at some length in previous books by the author (Horst, 1963, 1966). The importance of this concept as a starting point for all psychological as well as other scientific investigation is not generally recognized. Dimensionality is a fundamental concept in the most rigorous and elegant of all cognitive disciplines, namely, mathematics. Dimensionality is the basis for deciding what we are going to talk about or investigate. It is impossible to conduct any investigation without knowing the different aspects of whatever it is that we want to investigate. Any scientific investigation implies a data matrix of numbers in which the rows represent entities or things and the columns represent dimensions or attributes of these entities.

In *Psychological Measurement and Prediction* (Horst, 1966) we pointed out that no subject within a discipline can be adequately investigated without considering a number of different attributes. This concept would seem to be obvious and even trivial, yet the attributes or variables of a subject under investigation are often inadequately specified. If investigators do not adequately recognize the importance of dimensionality, their procedures may be confused and their results inconclusive.

We shall use more or less synonymously the terms "attributes," "characteristics," "variables," and "dimensions." The word "dimensions" has been used in the title of this book to emphasize the importance of dimensionality in personality measurement. In this chapter we shall attempt to develop the concept as it relates to the rationale and procedures appropriate for developing measures of personality. As a background for multidimensional personality measurement, we shall first discuss the role of attributes in psychological measurement in general. Then we shall consider single scale personality instruments, multiple scale instruments, and factor analysis as it relates to the subject of dimensionality.

ATTRIBUTES IN PSYCHOLOGICAL MEASUREMENT

Perhaps the easiest if not the best way to specify what one is going to talk about or investigate is to use a popular catchword or phrase such as *conservatism* or *authoritarianism* or *private initiative*. If one is a psychologist, he will not be at a loss to find catchy attribute labels such as *cognitive processes, rote learning, sensation, intelligence,* and last but not least, *personality.* If one decides to study personality or to construct a personality scale, he must decide whether to make a scale that measures just one aspect of personality or one that measures a number of things. We shall discuss the role of attributes in psychological measurement in terms of both single scales and multiple scales.

SINGLE SCALE PSYCHOLOGICAL INSTRUMENTS

Other things being equal, it is usually easier to talk about, think about, or work with, one thing at a time rather than a number of different things simultaneously. However, if one works with only one thing rather than a number of different things, he will doubtless overlook many things that are important. One way to eat one's cake and have it too is to call a lot of different things by a single name, and then forget or ignore that the single thing is actually a number of different things. General intelligence is an example. In spite of all the work done in the last three or four decades on the subject of intelligence and its measurement, there are still strong forces in academic and educational circles that regard intelligence as a single unitary thing.

The early work of Spearman (1927) in England, of Binet (1905) in France, and of Terman (1916) at Stanford was based on the assumption that intelligence was unitary. Measuring instruments were constructed which gave a single score for a person, and by a simple trick of arithmetic converted it to an IQ. Thus the well-known intelligence quotient was born and has had a vigorous existence ever since. In the early days of intelligence measurement, there was much discussion and argument about what intelligence is. The easy and question-begging answer was that intelligence is what the tests measure. Some, however, were not so easily satisfied with the idea that intelligence is a simple unidimensional phenomenon.

It is true, of course, that one can define a word in any way he wishes. If he is satisfied with his own definition, there is no further occasion for argument or controversy. However, the doubters were not convinced that the conception of intelligence as a simple unidimensional human phenomenon was consistent with observations of human behavior and adjustment. Even Spearman began to doubt his oversimplifications after analyzing intelligence test data. Soon Kelley (1935), Holzinger and Harman (1941), and Thurstone (1941) began seriously to attack the concept of intelligence as a unidimensional phenomenon, and contended that it could be more usefully conceived as multidimensional or a combination of a number of different attributes. The models they formulated and the experimental research they conducted on the basis of these models amply justified their contention.

Nevertheless, as late as 1964, the unidimensional concept of Spearman, Binet, and Terman was defended by McNemar (1964) in his presidential address at the annual meeting of the American Psychological Association. He summarized an impressive array of studies purporting to demonstrate the utility of the multidimensional concept of intelligence and attempted to reinterpret the results in terms of the unitary model.

But even among those who were early attracted by the simplicity of the IQ, some came to believe that intelligence was not everything. What about personality? This addition did not greatly complicate the problem of measuring and describing human behavior because it added only a second dimension, and fortunately, like intelligence, it had a label that had been in the public domain for centuries. If one could say of a person that he was intelligent and had a good personality, this was a pretty complete description. So in the early days the personality quotient or PQ was also offered to the lay public. However, the suspicion that human beings were not unidimensional or even just two-dimensional continued to nag many investigators. Personality, like intelligence, appeared to have more than one dimension, and the concept of the multidimensionality of human personality gradually received more and more attention.

MULTIPLE SCALES IN PSYCHOLOGICAL MEASUREMENT

We have already referred to the work of Kelley, Holzinger, and Thurstone which divides intelligence into a number of different attributes. The work of these investigators has been extensively reported in the literature, and in previous books we elaborated its significance (Horst, 1963, 1966a). The primary mental ability scales of Thurstone (1938) and even the earlier multidimensional scales of Thorndike (1927) exemplified the conviction that man is a many-faceted phenomenon rather than one that operates along a single line or within a plane. A cursory examination of the early intelligence scales of Binet (1905) and Terman (1916), and the later revised scales of Terman and Merrill (1937), revealed that the stimulus elements in the scale sampled many different kinds of behavior, including verbal, numerical, spatial, reasoning, perceptual, and other kinds of abilities or traits.

It also became obvious that the personality quotient greatly oversimplified the noncognitive behavior domain. Many attempts to measure different aspects of personality as a multidimensional phenomenon were made. Examples of these are the multiple scale Bernreuter Inventory (1935), the multiple scale Adjustment Inventory of Bell (1938), and the Minnesota Multiphasic Personality Inventory (Hathaway and Meehl, 1951).

SINGLE SCALE PERSONALITY MEASURES

We have discussed at some length at a general level the concepts of unidimensionality and multidimensionality as they relate to psychological measurement and in particular to personality measurement. We shall now consider in more detail some of the technical and procedural aspects involved in the single scale personality instrument. By a single scale instrument is meant one which yields a single score. Such a scale may be constructed from a set of items that are highly homogeneous, meaning that their covariances with one another are high so that the items tend to measure the same thing, whatever that thing might be. There are also single scale instruments in which the covariances among the items are not high. Whether homogeneous or heterogeneous, the collection of items should be such that logically or by some stretch of the imagination it may be given a single label.

HOMOGENEOUS PERSONALITY SCALES

The concept of homogeneity indicates the extent to which the items in a set measure the same thing. The homogeneity of a set of items may be experimentally determined by administering the items to a group of individuals, constructing a data matrix, and obtaining the minor product moment of this data matrix. In *Psychological Measurement and Prediction* (Horst, 1966a) we have shown how a raw covariance matrix may be transformed to a deviation covariance matrix, and finally to a correlation matrix. The elements of such a correlation matrix are known as phi coefficients if the items are dichotomously scored.

Methods for assembling a group of homogeneous items, called item analysis procedures, are described in many texts. There are many kinds of item analyses for many different purposes; these are discussed in *Psychological Measurement and Prediction* (Horst, 1966a). A most common type of analysis begins with a total test score which is the number of items answered correctly according to a prespecified key. Various indices may then be calculated to determine the degree of relationship of each item with the total score. It has been common practice to retain items which correlate high with the total score and reject those which do not. The criteria for deciding what is high and what is low are arbitrary and are usually at the discretion of the experimenter.

Curiously enough, this item selection procedure has been regarded by many over the years as a magic way of determining whether an item is good or bad. It has not been generally recognized that a procedure that selects items which correlate highly with the total score achieves a very limited objective. This principle of item selection tends to select items which are highly correlated among themselves and therefore homogeneous by definition.

It is also important to recognize that as one eliminates items from the total pool, the scores resulting from the remaining items are not in general the same as those obtained from the total pool of items. The item-test correlations, or other indices of relationship, will also change as the set on which the total score is based is reduced or altered. The method of selecting items which correlate high with total test scores is useful primarily if the major objective is to select a group of homogeneous items.

The Kuder-Richardson (1937) formula 20 for estimating reliability gives an estimate of reliability which is an increasing function of the item-test correlations. The higher these correlations, the higher the Kuder-Richardson reliability estimate. The appropriateness of the Kuder-Richardson formula for estimating test reliability may be questioned, but it can be useful as an index of the homogeneity of the test items. Test reliability, as determined by retest procedures, will increase—other things being equal—as the homogeneity of the items increases.

One of the difficulties with using the item-test correlation procedure for selecting items for a homogeneous personality test is that there is no correct answer in general for the personality type test item. One must arbitrarily or by some prespecified experimental design determine the keyed answer for some given objective and then score the total group of items according to such a key. Procedures are available for establishing keyed answers so that total test scores may be calculated for use in item homogeneity analysis. For example, one of the simplest is to designate as the keyed answer to a personality item the one marked by most people. Edwards (1957) has shown in the case of two-choice or dichotomous response sets that answers selected by most people also tend to be the socially desirable responses. For multiple-response element sets the problem of determining the *correct* answer as a basis for getting total scores is more complicated than for two-response element sets. In any case, it is doubtful whether it is worth while to conduct conventional type homogeneity analyses for the construction of single scale personality tests. Multiple scale tests have much more to recommend them, and the analytical and computational procedures developed in later chapters do not depend greatly on homogeneous subsets of items.

HETEROGENEOUS ITEMS IN SINGLE PERSONALITY SCALES

One approach in the construction of a single dimension personality scale is to disregard the question of whether or not the items have high intercorrelations. This is in contrast to the item analysis procedures for the construction of single scale personality instruments which employ such indices of item-test relationship as covariances, biserial or point biserial correlations, or other cruder measures of relationship between item and total test score. In some cases, personality tests have been constructed largely from rational considerations alone. Items such as might be found in typical psychiatric or psychoanalytic interviews have been grouped together and with very little justification called a personality test. However, there are instances where single scale personality instruments might with some justification be constructed without the benefit of item homogeneity analyses. For example, one may consistently observe certain behavior phenomena, such as the tendency to become anxious in test or examination situations. This phenomenon has come to be generally recognized over the years as a concomitant of test-taking situations. One may therefore postulate or hypothesize an attribute which he decides to call test anxiety. He may then construct or collect a number of items which he believes will indicate whether persons tend to develop anxieties when taking tests, even though the items may cover a wide variety of behavior phenomena. Such single scale instruments may be useful for diagnostic, prognostic, and therapeutic purposes.

So also one may postulate that some persons have a tendency to say "yes" and others "no" to statements for which the alternative responses are negation or affirmation. This tendency may be postulated as a personality trait. One may wish to construct a test in which the item content is irrelevant and for which the score is merely the number of "yes" answers. Such a scale will almost surely not consist of highly homogeneous items. Scores from such a test might be useful if it is found that for a wide variety of stimulus elements some persons have consistent tendencies to respond "yes" and others "no," irrespective of the particular stimulus elements presented to them.

One may also observe that some persons have a greater than average tendency to give the socially desirable response to a group of items, irrespective of how the items apply to them. This tendency was discussed in the previous chapter. One may, then, postulate a tendency to give socially desirable responses, and may assemble a group of items scaled for social desirability. The primary criterion in assembling these items may be that they exhibit a wide range of variation in their social desirability scale values. The correct answer then to each of such a group of dichotomously scored items will be the socially desirable answer. The persons with the highest scores are those who tend to give socially desirable answers. Here again is an example of a single scale that is not concerned with the homogeneity of the items. As a matter of fact, it may be desirable that such a collection be as heterogeneous as possible so that other aspects of behavior will tend to cancel one another.

Some groups of items that have been assembled for single scale tests do not necessarily represent such clearly demonstrable phenomena as test anxiety, acquiescence, or social desirability. Some investigators prefer to use their own rational judgment as to what kinds of items should go into a scale, how they should be phrased, and what particular areas of behavior they should sample, rather than to be guided by quantitative and statistical characteristics of scores resulting from the administration of the tests. Even today, some psychologists place a great deal of reliance on rational and so-called logical procedures for arriving at hypotheses about which behavior or personality variables are in some way real and fundamental. The personality systems developed by Freud (1938), Jung (1933), Adler (1927), and others are of this rationalistic kind and may be sharply distinguished from those based on more scientific approaches. While the rational approach to the measurement of personality variables may be scholarly and display a high order of art, it should not be confused with the scientific approach.

Some investigators maintain that the kinds of rationalization and construct development used by the early pioneers and their disciples in the formulation of personality systems are a part of the scientific method in that such activities properly precede the experimental, quantitative, and analytical approaches. This is not the place to discuss the philosophy of science or methodological epistemology in general. It may be that scientific investigations may profit from the use of rationalizations, intervening variables, and hypothetical constructs, but it has not been convincingly demonstrated that these are a necessary part of the scientific method. It is possible, for example, to assemble a very large collection of many different types of behavior items without having any hypotheses about personality structure or the organization of human behavior, and by purely statistical and computational procedures achieve useful and definitive objective results.

It is true, of course, that the informal collection, analysis, and interpretation of data generated by previous events may be regarded as hypothesis formation activities. As such, they may be considered preliminary to more formal experimental and analytical procedures.

LABELING PROCESS

For a single scale personality instrument, the labeling of the scale may assume considerable importance, at least in the eyes of the investigator. We have seen how labels might evolve during observations of psychological testing activities—for example, when people are taking tests, repeated manifestations of behavior may be observed which might be called anxiety. The term "anxiety" is common in both lay terminology and in the professional jargon of psychologists, psychiatrists, and others concerned with the normal and abnormal behavior of people. It is natural, then, that such a term be adopted as one of widespread significance and interest for human beings in general and for personality measurement in particular. So also, in the case of "acquiescence" and "social desirability," not only do informal observations lead to the conclusion that these may be useful, meaningful, and relatively unambiguous labels for easily and frequently recognized types of behavior, but such conclusions may also be supported by scientifically and competently designed experimental investigations.

In the personality field, not all labels generated to designate personality scales have been so generally recognized and verified by psychologists as those we have mentioned. Many labels used by those working in the field of personality measurement or in clinical psychology have had their origin in the language of the layman. For example, such expressions as "hostility," "aggression," "frustration," "sociability," and so on, have come directly from the literature of the ages and the man on the street. This is not to say that they may not appropriately be used to tie together useful and meaningful sets of concepts and behavior manifestations. Actually, they may be so used, and perhaps even more appropriately because their persistence in the language may signify fundamental aspects of the behavior of human beings as they react with one another.

Labels can play a useful role both as a basis for initiating investigations into more accurate formulations of personality dimensions and for the communication of important social concepts within a collective society. Nevertheless, there is always the danger that long established labels may create unjustified confidence in the labeled instruments simply because a well-known and trusted name has been given them.

Most single scale personality instruments probably started out with labels which have more or less meaning for many persons and perhaps greater meaning and significance for the originators. The label appears to be the most logical starting place for anyone who wishes to develop a single score personality scale. One then proceeds to collect stimulus elements that will evoke responses presumed to constitute the set of stimulus-response patterns which may appropriately be given the name of the chosen label.

ITEMS IN THE PERSONALITY SCALE

One may assemble at random any group of items he wishes from the vast number which have been developed over the past decades, and print them together according to some format, but ordinarily for a single scale test he begins with a label and attempts to find items which he regards as belonging appropriately under that label. Very little systematic work has been done in developing structured procedures and specifications for collecting or developing a set of items that will measure a particular labeled personality variable. Flanagan (1949) and his students developed an item rationale technique as a basis for item construction. In the early days of objective measurement, much more attention was paid to specifications and techniques for developing items for a particular purpose than has been the case in recent years. For example, Ruch's (1929) early work in this field is a classic. The work of Bloom (1956) and others on taxonomy of educational objectives is relevant to structured procedures for the development of test items for specific purposes.

Most of these techniques have been used as a basis for developing instructional methods as well as scales to measure either vocational or educational achievement. For example, many years ago the Procter and Gamble Company developed a procedure for writing training manuals. It began with job analyses, task analyses, and difficulty analyses, and concluded with solution analyses. Such a procedure can also provide the basis for the rational development of test items, but surprisingly enough, it has not been used for this purpose.

The "critical incidents" technique of Flanagan (1954) is relevant for vocational objectives concerned with the development of selection tests or the preparation of evaluation instruments for the selection of airplane pilots or the evaluation of medical interns or military officers. These techniques may be applied in almost any field of endeavor, but to date their use has been restricted essentially to well-defined areas of career or vocational activity. The techniques, which result in a large collection of incidents or situations in which adequate performance is crucial to success in the activity, have provided the basis for item construction.

The procedures available for the development of a scale to measure hostility, for example, are not as well defined. One may collect a large number of items that are regarded as exhibiting behavior called "hostility" in specific situations. In the same way, one can take any other label, such as sociability or dependence, and formulate as specifically and concretely as possible a number of behavior items that define that trait. Presumably, one might also submit his list of items to a group of authorities for criticism. These experts could be asked to indicate items that should be eliminated from the set because they do not typify the kind of thing implied by the label, or to suggest other items that would be typical of the characteristic to be measured. By such procedures, one might arrive at a group of items which may with some degree of confidence be thought to measure the characteristic the investigator is interested in.

It is doubtful whether much work and effort is justified in attempts to develop personality items to measure a particular hypothesized trait to which a more or less arbitrary label is assigned. In the first place, one may question the procedures by which the labels are arrived at as a basis for developing a scale. In the second place, one may question the adequacy with which the more or less vague procedures discussed will result in a group of items that do measure a real personality or behavior variable.

One problem is to define the term "real." This problem has plagued psychologists and social scientists for many years. One would not be so naïve as to ask whether there "really" is such a thing as aggression, hostility, sociability, and so forth. Such questions could not be answered without recourse to more philosophical approaches to the meaning of reality. It is highly questionable whether speculations in this direction would be fruitful. We may, however, ask in what respect the items generated by labels may assist usefully in the confirmation or modification of labels that will in some sense exhibit scientifically or practically useful properties. These properties and the criteria for testing the utility and validity of labels will be considered either explicitly or implicitly in the following chapters. We shall see that the single scale implies relatively unsophisticated concepts about the nature of measurement and human personality. Ultimately the particular items employed in an investigation suggest labels for the scales which we purport to have developed, but except for purposes of communication, the labels for these scales are not of great importance.

MULTIPLE SCALES

In the previous section we discussed the construction of single scale personality measures and suggested that, except for special cases and purposes, the single scale approach is probably not the best way to measure personality. Because of the limitations of the single scale approach, the tendency has been to develop multiple scales within a single instrument. Personality inventories of this type are designed to yield a number of different scores such that each score gives the measure for a single personality trait or dimension.

Various approaches to the development of multiple scale personality inventories have been used. One approach makes use of rational or a priori hypotheses about the dimensions or variables that we wish to measure. A statistically more sophisticated method of developing multiple scales is to specify a number of socially significant criterion variables which we hope the scales will help predict. Whatever the basis for specifying the variables to be measured by the scales, several methods are available for accomplishing this with a pool of personality type items. One method is to segregate groups of items such that each subgroup purports to measure a single criterion variable. Another, more general, method is to assume that various ways of scoring the items can be developed such that from each scoring method a particular criterion variable can be estimated. A more general approach to the development of multiple scales is the factor analytical approach which avoids many of the problems we have discussed.

Whatever methods are used to define the set of variables to be measured by a multiple scale instrument, and whatever the procedure for deriving scale scores from the instruments, one should begin with some notion of the rough order of magnitude of the total number of factors that might be usefully measured.

RATIONAL SCALES

In the past, rational multiple scales have been developed largely on the basis of personality theory, arrived at for the most part through a priori or philosophical ruminations. Perhaps one of the best examples of a rational approach to the development of personality dimensions is that of Henry Murray (1938) in his classic study of needs. Murray's work provided the basis for the dimensions postulated in the Edward's Personal Preference Schedule (1957), and to date there appears to be no better or more convincing a priori labeling of personality traits than these. The listing provided by Murray of twenty-four labeled and defined traits also provided the basis for a study by Campbell (1959) on dimensions of personality. Because the phenomena discussed and studied by Murray were called "needs," labels that are based on the work of Murray are referred to as "needs" rather than "personality traits." However, when one examines the various kinds of statements and behavior situations developed by those who attempt to measure Murray's needs, they appear similar to the vast number of personality type items that have been employed over the past to measure various aspects of interests, preferences, adjustment, temperament, and other personality areas.

By now it would be difficult to invent or write a set of items most of which have not already been included in some previously published set. Most new items will vary only slightly from some that have already been produced. In any case, let us assume that in some manner one has assembled a large pool of items, whether new or old. One may either segregate subsets of those items that seem to go together and give well-known and popularly accepted names to them, or start with a set of hypothetical variables and attempt to sort the items according to this predetermined set of labels. The labels may be arrived at by elaborate theoretical rationalizations or other methods, some of which have been suggested in previous sections of this chapter.

CRITERION SCALES

A more empirical approach to the construction of personality type scales can be taken by specifying a number of different activities within social institutions, such as schools, industry, and the military services. The preparation or segregation of items used to measure or predict success in these various defined fields of social activity may use a wide variety of more or less sophisticated and adequate procedures. The method used in the well-known Strong Vocational Interest Blank (1943) was to develop separate scoring procedures for each of a large number of vocational and occupational activities.

The criterion approach to the development of personality scales is entirely different from the rational approach. It is purely empirical. Very little theorizing or rationalizing is involved in labeling the scales; the labels are predetermined by contemporary social institutions. Whatever the validity or utility of the labeling of human activities within the major institutions of our society, these labels are in large part the basis of the criterion type multiple personality scales.

The multiple criterion type scale lends itself to a bewilderingly large number of possible scales for any given multidimensional enterprise. For example, if one wished to develop a multiple scale to measure all criterion variables corresponding to job activities listed in the *Dictionary of Occupational Titles,* he would have many thousands of scales in a single instrument. This is, of course, an extreme case, but it suggests the vast number of pseudodimensions that might be generated by unbridled attempts to develop criterion scales. As a matter of fact, studies with the Minnesota Multiphasic Personality Inventory (Hathaway and Meehl, 1951) have already generated several hundred different criterion scales. In the next chapter we shall consider in greater detail some of the more technical aspects of the criterion multiple scale approach, as well as some of its limitations.

UNIQUE SCORING FOR MULTIPLE SCALES

For both rational and criterion scales, several strategies of scoring may be considered. One of these consists simply in scoring a subset of items for each of the specified scales. The manner in which these subsets are determined and allocated to the particular rational or criterion scale will be discussed in more detail in the next chapter. However, if for each scale we have a unique set of items to be scored for that scale, then the larger the number of scales in the instrument the greater the number of items that will be required. We know from elementary psychological measurement theory that we cannot in general get reliable measures of a single variable with only a few items. Therefore we must assume that the unique subset procedure for constructing multiple scales will give a reasonable number of items in each subset, perhaps not less than twelve. Assuming at least twelve items to a scale, it is obvious that if we have a multiple scale involving as many as 100 alleged dimensions, a total of 1200 items would be required. This implies an inventory of rather frightening proportions. It is true that in experimental studies subjects have been paid to answer a set of up to 3000 items. Such a project requires a number of successive sittings for each subject. If one hopes within one sitting to obtain all of the measures implied by a large number of labeled scales with uniquely segregated subsets of items, the enterprise would appear to be impractical.

This dilemma implies a criticism of both the unrestricted number of alleged scales for a given instrument and the principle of unique segregation of subsets of items for the measurement of each dimension. Of course, it would be possible to have a separate test for each labeled scale so that one could have perhaps up to a fifty-item test for measuring each of the assumed dimensions. The confusion the testing movement has brought about in our educational and other social institutions would be greatly compounded if the market should become flooded with a thousand different tests, each with fifty or 100 items, to represent all of the labels that skilled verbalists could invent. The solution to this dilemma is probably to restrict very rigorously the total number of scales and also to use multiple duty items, or items which function in more than one of the scales.

ALTERNATIVE SCORING PROCEDURES

We may have subsets of items that are not unique, that is, subsets that overlap so that some items in one set are also included in another. One could then have a much larger number of subsets than is the case when an item appears in only one set. Such a procedure, however, is not recommended. Other things being equal, the greater the amount of overlapping of items among the subsets, the higher will be the correlations among the scores yielded by the subsets. As overlapping increases, the intercorrelations will approach unity and the scores cannot provide differentiation among the alleged criterion or rational variables.

The difficulties implied by this discussion result from the assumption that the items appearing in more than one subset are keyed the same for all subsets in which they occur. An alternative is to score differently items which appear in several subsets. For example, suppose that the items are dichotomously scored. One response may be keyed for some of the subsets in which an item appears and the other response for the other subsets in which it appears. By appropriate alternation of the keyed responses of the various items in the total pool, one could still generate scale scores in which the correlations among the scores were not undesirably high.

In the case of multiple choice response alternatives and sets of ideal weighting vectors with differential elements, even more flexibility is possible in the generation of scale scores that would exhibit low intercorrelations. For example, with appropriate determinations of these differential sets of weights, one could obtain scores which exhibit high reliability and maximum dispersion and at the same time result in relatively low intercorrelations among the scores. The limits of such optimal statistical characteristics would be determined by the particular items included and the particular strategies of defining or specifying the scales themselves. We shall have more to say about this feature of differential scoring in Chapter 4. We shall also exploit it further in the procedural developments of later chapters.

FACTOR TYPE SCALES

A third type of scale which has attracted much attention and provided the basis for the development of a number of multiple scale instruments is based on factor analytic techniques. The term "factor analysis" has come to be well known in psychology because the technique was developed by psychologists. The technique has now been applied in many other academic disciplines. Factor analytic techniques provide a useful basis for specifying and defining objectively the dimensions of any system under investigation, whether it be in a particular area of psychology such as personality or in other disciplines.

NUMBERS OF DIMENSIONS HYPOTHESIZED

In the development of a multidimensional scale a hypothesis

as to the total number of dimensions that may usefully be investigated is implied. Unfortunately, most investigations of psychologists and other social scientists imply that the total number of variables within the field is limitless. Hence a preoccupation of researchers is to find new variables to investigate on the assumption that there always will be new ones, no matter how many have already been defined or labeled. This point of view encourages the unfortunate practice of giving new labels to old things and thereby confusing the literature with needlessly proliferated terminology. In the cases of both rational and criterion scales, it seems imperative that the field of investigation be so structured and the hypotheses so formulated as to restrict in advance the total number of usefully investigatable dimensions. The factor analytic techniques help to determine objectively the total number of variables within a segment of the domain of investigation, but for computational convenience we shall see that we need to postulate some upper limit to this total number.

FACTOR ANALYSIS

In the physical sciences a relatively small number of variables suffice for the analysis and prediction of physical phenomena. In chemistry we have a limited number of chemical elements as the basis for describing the vast number of chemical compounds and substances found in nature. In the biological sciences the number of variables involved is not so limited as in the physical sciences, but the physiologists agree reasonably well on variables that can be used as a basis for describing biological phenomena.

In the social sciences, however, and in psychology in particular, the situation is quite different. Psychologists have not been able to agree on a limited set of fundamental variables that appear even reasonably adequate as a basis for the description, analysis, and prediction of most of the important aspects of human behavior.

It is all very well to say that each investigator may define his variables in any way he pleases, and devise methods for measuring them. The difficulty is, of course, that if each psychologist chooses or defines his own variables without respect to the way other psychologists select and define theirs, the inevitable outcome will be a vast conglomeration of unorganized, unstructured variables which, far from clarifying our understanding of human behavior, only serve further to confuse it. In this section we shall discuss in more detail the important methodology of factor analysis, since it can play such a crucial role in psychological measurement and in the definition of the things measured. We shall discuss the nature and purpose of factor analysis, the various kinds of factors, and the relationship between factors and tests.

NATURE AND PURPOSE OF FACTOR ANALYSIS

Factor analysis typically begins with a matrix of measures for a sample of entities on a number of different attributes or variables. These variables may be the items in a personality test. Such a matrix, of course, implies that the variables are already available and that the techniques or instrumentations for measuring them have been developed. It may be difficult to see how factor analysis can be useful in defining or specifying the fundamental variables of psychology when it cannot begin to operate before these have already been specified. We shall see that factor analysis can be useful in defining or specifying the fundamental variables of a discipline— whether psychology or any other—only after some a priori hypotheses have already been made as to what these variables are. But this is not a serious limitation.

Typically a factor analysis begins with a correlation matrix. Each correlation coefficient indicates the degree of relationship between two variables in a particular sample. The correlation matrix can be derived from a matrix of multiple measures such as personality item scores for a sample of persons. This matrix is a convenient way to summarize the relationships among the particular variables. However, a correlation matrix can be difficult to interpret because of the large number of correlation coefficients.

If we have a correlation matrix of 100 variables or test items, the total number of intercorrelations will be large. The formula for this number is given by $n(n-1)/2$, so that for 100 items the total number of correlations is 4950. For 200 items this number is 19,900.

It must therefore be obvious that even for a table of intercorrelations with much less than 100 variables, it would be difficult to interpret all of the relationships. Such large numbers of correlations can be difficult to interpret because of the redundancy among the measures. The higher the correlation among variables in a set of multiple measures, the greater the redundancy in the definition and measurement of the variables to be measured.

The fact that psychologists invent or define many different things to measure and relate to one another is not of itself objectionable. If in general the correlations among the things measured were low, there would be scientific justification for measuring them separately. If the variables are reliably measured and the correlations among them are low, they may be regarded as measuring independent aspects of human behavior, and therefore each would be uniquely relevant to the study of human behavior. That such independence is not typical has been repeatedly demonstrated by matrices of intercorrelations.

In general, a major objective of all the sciences is to describe phenomena in terms of a smaller number of basic or fundamental variables. In the social sciences the number of observable phenomena which we attempt to describe in terms of a much smaller number of basic variables is much greater than in the physical sciences. The dimensionality of a matrix of measures is the number of these basic variables necessary to account for the observed measures within a specified degree of accuracy. If we have scores on a large number of different tests for each of a number of persons, we may find a much smaller number of basic variables to account for the scores on the observed tests. These basic variables are called factors. If we have a correlation matrix for a large number of observed measures and it is possible to express the measures in terms of a smaller number of factors, it is also possible to solve from the observed correlation matrix for a factor loading matrix in terms of which we can reproduce the correlation matrix by appropriate methods of analysis. To understand how such a factor loading matrix can be found, a familiarity with simple matrix algebra and with the basic elements of factor analysis are necessary. These are available in *Matrix Algebra for Social Scientists* (Horst, 1963) and *Factor Analysis of Data Matrices* (Horst, 1965).

We may consider a factor loading matrix with as many columns as there are factors, and as many rows as tests. We may then solve for the elements of such a matrix so that the major product moment of this matrix gives an adequate approximation to the correlation matrix. The first step in a factor analysis of a correlation matrix is to determine the minimum number of factors that can adequately account for the correlation matrix. By mathematical and statistical means we can determine how many factors are required to account for the correlation matrix within some specified degree of approximation.

If one factor loading matrix can be found whose major product moment* approximates the correlation matrix with a pre-specified degree of accuracy, then an infinite number of different factor loading matrices may be found whose major product moments give precisely the same matrix. The basic mathematics underlying this concept involves orthogonal transformations. Thurstone (1947) provided a method, which he called the simple structure concept, for overcoming this indeterminancy in factor analytic procedures. He considered the problem of finding, from all of the infinitely large number of possible factor loading matrices which adequately reproduce the correlation matrix, that particular one which may in some sense be said to be the primary factor loading matrix.

The concept of simple structure applies to the factor loading matrix, which consists of numbers such that each number corresponds to a given factor and test. For each test, therefore, we have a number corresponding to each factor, and for each factor a number for each test. These numbers may be positive, negative, or zero. What they are depends largely on the particular method of solving for the factor loading matrix. To get a unique solution the simple structure criteria are used. One of these is the positive manifold.

---

* Unless otherwise specified, a *major product moment* of a matrix is the product of a vertical matrix postmultiplied by its transpose, and a *minor product moment* is a vertical matrix premultiplied by its transpose. (See Horst, 1963.)

Other things being equal, the factor loading matrix should have a minimum number of negative factor loadings. But for many factor loading matrices corresponding to particular correlation matrices, we may still have an infinite number of factor loading matrices which have mostly positive factor loadings. To further restrict the selection of the particular matrix, we require also that each column shall have a small number of high factor loadings and a large number of near-zero factor loadings. We also require that each row of the factor loading matrix shall have at least one near-zero factor loading, and that at least one of the others shall be large positive. Furthermore, for every pair of factors, not many tests shall have high loadings in both. Also, for any pair of factors, a number of tests shall have high loadings in one factor and near-zero in another. Finally, a pair of factors shall have a large number of zero loadings for both factors.

According to these criteria, if we plot the factor loadings of one factor against those of another, a number of tests would cluster about zero, others would be high on one axis and low on the other, and others low on the former and high on the latter. The extent to which these criteria of simple structure can be found depends on the particular variables involved in the experiment. In any case, a procedure for finding the best simple structure matrix for any given set of variables gives an indication of which variables are the best measures for which factors. The factors can then be defined in terms of the variables that have relatively high loadings on them.

Thurstone hypothesized that the simple structure criteria should enable one to identify factors that make what he called "psychological sense." There is rather general agreement that factors defined on the basis of simple structure procedures do make psychological sense. Such agreement is of considerable importance for effective communication.

KINDS OF FACTORS

There is still considerable disagreement as to which types of factors should be postulated in a satisfactory analysis of correlation matrices. Originally Spearman (1927) postulated two kinds of factors, a general factor and specific factors. Spearman was most interested in the general factor. He observed that in matrices of correlation coefficients there tended to be high correlations among measures obtained with currently available psychological tests. He assumed that a general factor of intelligence "caused" the correlation among the factors.

In addition to this general factor of intelligence, Spearman hypothesized specific factors for each of the tests. Each test then was characterized by its loading on the general factor and on a specific factor peculiar to that test. This model was extended by Thurstone (1947) to include not only specific factors but also a number of common factors. In the Spearman model there was only one common factor—the general factor of intelligence.

Thurstone developed computational procedures for finding more than one common factor, provided more than one factor was required to account adequately for the intercorrelations. The common factors were defined as common to at least two, and preferably more, of the tests in the battery, while a specific factor had loadings in only one test.

There is some confusion as to the distinction between general and common factors. A general factor is ordinarily thought of as one on which all of the tests have loadings, while a common factor is one on which some but not all of the tests have loadings. These are not precise specifications because in any arithmetic solution we do not get precisely zero loadings in any of the factors. For all factors, most tests have at least slight positive or negative loadings. These concepts have been unfortunately confused in the literature, and further clarification of them is needed. Even so, factor analysis provides the best objective procedures available for defining the dimensions of a system.

The specific factor model gets us into difficulty because it postulates not only common and perhaps general factors fewer in number than the number of variables, but also as many specific factors as variables. Thus the model which includes specific factors generates more factor variables than the number of variables from which these factors were derived. Another difficulty is the fact that what is specific in one battery may become common in another. If a battery includes two tests which measure almost the same thing but are very different from all of the other tests, we may get a common factor for these two tests and zero loadings on this factor for all of the other tests. On the other hand, if we omit one of the two tests, then in that battery we get only a specific factor for the remaining test since all of the other tests have zero loadings on this factor.

It is not in general possible to account exactly for all of the measures in a data matrix of multiple measures, or for the correlations in the correlation matrix derived from such a data matrix, without solving for as many factors as there are variables. It is only because we assume that there are random or unsystematic components to the various measures that we are entitled to approximate rather than reproduce the correlation matrix. We can choose this approximation so that the number of factors will be less than the number of variables. If we do, then it is necessary also to consider additional factors that are required to account for the discrepancies between the approximation and the correlation matrix. These we call error factors.

The proponents of specific factors have not made clear what are error and what are specific factors. In any case, the error factors make the approximate or estimated correlations either higher or lower than the observed correlations. In general, they will not make the diagonal elements larger than unity. One of the important conditions to be satisfied by any factor analytic model is that the sum of the squares of the factor loadings for a particular test equals the variance of that test. If the variance is unity, as in the case of the correlation matrix, then the sum of the squares of all factor loadings for that test, including general, common, specific, and error, must total to unity.

FACTORS AND TESTS

We have said that factor analysis can be useful in helping to determine, from among a large group of psychological measures, which of them may be regarded as measures of pure factors. The

simple structure procedures have as their primary objective the iden-
tification of those variables in a battery which are the best measures
of the factors represented by the battery. After the simple structure
factor loading matrix has been calculated, those tests with the highest loadings in each factor are defined as the best measures of that
factor. If a test has a high loading in one factor and zero loadings
in all of the others, and if it has little error variance, then we may
regard that test as a relatively pure measure of the factor. However,
in most factor analytic studies no single test has zero loadings on
all but one factor. But if a test has a high loading on one factor and
much smaller loadings on all of the other factors, we still regard it
as a relatively pure measure of the factor.

We are now in a position to distinguish between two important types of multiple measure sets. The first of these is a set of
measures collected on some a priori or rational basis. Such sets of
multiple measures may contain large numbers of variables, whether
consisting of individual items or of sets of such items which we call
tests or scales. We have seen that it is difficult to summarize information yielded by measures from such arbitrary or a priori sets. The
alternative is to substitute for such sets a much smaller number of
pure factor measures providing essentially the same information.
These pure factor measures constitute the second of the two important types of multiple measure sets.

We shall now consider more specifically the meaning of a factor loading. If the factor analysis is performed on the correlation
matrix, which is usually the case, the factor loading of a test on a
particular factor is the correlation of that test with the factor.
Therefore, a factor loading must lie between -1 and $+1$. If the
analysis is performed on a covariance matrix, then the factor loadings are covariances of the tests with the factors. Each test has a
correlation or a covariance with every factor. If we had pure measures of the factors represented by a battery of tests, then the factor
loadings would be precisely the correlations of the tests with these
pure factor tests.

Test scores could be regarded as weighted combinations of
factor scores, provided factor scores were available on each factor

for each of a group of individuals. The score on a particular test would be a linear combination of the scores on the factors. In the case of personality items, the item scores would be a linear combination of the scores on the personality factors. There would be such a linear combination for each test. The weighting vectors for the linear combinations will differ, of course, from one test to another. The matrix of factor loadings is actually the matrix of the weighting vectors.

Equations 3.1 and 3.2 show in scalar notation how we express a test score as a weighted sum of factor scores.

$$X_{ij} = Y_{i1}\, a_{1j} + U_{i2}\, a_{2j} + \cdots + Y_{im}\, a_{mj} + \epsilon_{ij} \tag{3.1}$$

$$X_{ij} = \sum_{k=1}^{m} Y_{ik}\, a_{kj} + \epsilon_{ij} \tag{3.2}$$

where

m is the number of factors,
X_{ij} is the test score of the ith person on the jth test,
Y_{ik} is the factor score of the ith person on the kth factor,
a_{kj} is the factor loading of the jth test on the kth factor, and
ϵ_{ij} is a residual test score which may have a specific component, depending on the model used.

Equation 3.3 shows in matrix notation how the complete test score matrix may be expressed as the product of a matrix of factor scores and a matrix of factor loadings.

$$X = Ya' + \epsilon \tag{3.3}$$

where

X is an $N \times n$ matrix of test scores,
Y is an $N \times m$ matrix of factor scores,
a' is an $m \times n$ matrix of factor loadings, and
ϵ is an $N \times n$ matrix of residual scores.

If we have given a factor loading matrix derived from a correlation matrix, and also the test score matrix, we can solve for the factor score matrix. Procedures for doing this are outlined in *Factor Anal-*

ysis of Data Matrices (Horst, 1965). The solution for this factor score matrix is such that when substituted in Equation 3.3 we get an approximation to the test score matrix. If we have as many factors as tests, we can get an exact solution to the test score matrix. However, we would have achieved no parsimony in the description of the observed data.

CHAPTER 4

Kinds of Multiple Scales

*I*n the previous chapter we considered briefly the major types of multiple scales for personality measurement. Now, as a basis for a comparison of these various kinds of scales, we shall consider them in more detail, discussing first the more primitive random scale model, and then elaborating on rational scales, criterion scales, and factor scales.

RANDOM SCALES

One could begin the construction of a multiple scale inventory without any hypotheses as to what he wants to measure. The assembling of the items should not be difficult. As has been indicated in Chapter 3, the test constructor has already available to him a great wealth of personality type items from which to make his selections. By now, the important contribution to be made in personality measurement lies in the development and utilization of more sophisticated mathematical, statistical, and computational techniques, rather than in the further proliferation of personality type item statements.

One could now, by means of a table of random numbers or some comparable procedure, group the items selected into subsets having no rational significance. This procedure may appear naïve but it has been effectively used by Hase and Goldberg (1966) in a most interesting study designed to compare the validity of different strategies of constructing personality scales. These investigators constructed four sets of multiple scales from a large pool of personality items; one of these was a set of random scales and the other three sets were rational, criterion, and factor scales.

Actually, the authors differentiated two types of rational scales. One they called the rational intuitive scale. Here the investigator presumably has some dimension or personality trait in mind when he attempts to select items which he believes will relate to the dimension. In this method, the test constructor depends upon his own intuition in understanding the dimension to be assessed and no formal psychological theory is purportedly followed. In the second rational scale, which the authors call the rational theoretical approach, a formal psychological theory is used as a guide to test construction. In actual practice it is difficult to differentiate between these two strategies. In the first case the test constructor uses his own more or less formal psychological theory, while in the latter case he uses that of someone else.

Hase and Goldberg used the results from the set of random scales as a basis for comparing the results from the rational, criterion, and factor scales. They presumably assumed that random scales would give very poor results according to a number of logical and acceptable criteria of multiple scale effectiveness, and that the scales which gave the best results on these same criteria would constitute the preferred strategy of scale construction. If none of the other three types gave better results than the random scales, then they might assume that either the random scale procedure should be employed or that there was no reason to bother with multiple scales. As a matter of fact, they found that rational, criterion, and factor scales all gave better results than the random scales.

RATIONAL SCALES

We have already discussed the subject of rational scales in general and some of the details involved in their construction. In this section, we shall give special attention to the determination of the attributes, the preparation of the behavior statements themselves, and the procedure as a background for constructing both criterion and factor scales.

DETERMINING THE ATTRIBUTES

In the light of our previous discussions, one may question whether there is much point in elaborate a priori efforts to formulate a set of labels presumed to measure the important dimensions of personality. However, such a classificatory exercise can be useful in most scientific activities in providing perspective for the undertaking so that appropriate emphasis can be given to relevant aspects of the domain being investigated. Attempts to rationalize and set down essential rubrics of the domain may enable one more equitably to distribute emphasis to the various classificatory subdivisions and help to prevent overlooking attributes that may be important. The preparation of a tentative set of attributes in a test development enterprise serves very much the same function as the preparation of an outline before writing an article or a book—such an exercise can be useful in organizing one's thinking and activities. The question is not so much whether by such a priori efforts the best set of attributes in some absolute sense has been formulated as whether a set has been found which will enable the investigator to cover most of the essential dimensions of personality, even if these are confounded, overlapping, or otherwise not as clear-cut as later research will help to make them.

There are now so many personality theories and proposals

about the dimensions of personality that the investigator may well supplement his own list with previously developed lists such as Murray's (1938). He can then direct his efforts toward eliminating redundancies and clarifying ambiguities.

BEHAVIOR STATEMENTS

With the set of labels decided upon, the investigator may construct or use previously formulated personality statements in compiling groups of items for each of his labels. Collecting a large enough number of these items should present no difficulty.

However, little is known about the form which personality statements should take—whether they should be impersonal or in the first person, be complete sentences, be well polished from the point of view of grammar and diction or phrased colloquially. It is probable that complete sentences, more or less colloquial and in the first person, may be more meaningful and easier for the subject to identify himself with than more formal and impersonal statements. We pointed out earlier the importance in personality questionnaires of having the subject structure himself as a part of the stimulus element for each item. Any techniques, tricks, or methods that can better achieve the integration of the item with the responding individual should result in more accurate and valid measures.

It is perhaps not crucial that each of the dimensions postulated be adequately represented by a sample of items. Most a priori sets of postulated behavior or personality dimensions are probably not very close to those which the objective methods of classification now available will yield. Nor is it highly probable that most of the behavior statements will be allocated by objective analysis techniques to the attribute categories they were designed to measure.

BACKGROUND FOR CRITERION SCALES

If one has available a large pool of personality type items from which to develop a set of multiple criterion scales, the statistical and methodological procedures are fairly straightforward. One may start out, for example, with a set of MMPI items and develop procedures for grouping them into subsets for estimating criterion values. This approach assumes that one has already decided on a set of criterion variables and that he wishes to estimate as accurately as possible each of these criteria with the pool of items.

On the other hand, one may adopt some rational or a priori approach to the selection of a pool of items from already available sources, or he may use these rational categories as the basis for developing his own items. These two methods may of course be used in combination.

One can also combine the rational and the criterion scale approach. For example, one may develop a multiple rational scale instrument based on theories or intuitions such that the scale yields a score for each of the hypothesized dimensions. This rational scale approach can be followed up with the criterion scale approach discussed in the next section. Procedures are available for combining scores from the rational scale to estimate each of a number of pre-specified criterion variables. In such a procedure the data matrix of item responses is first multiplied by a scoring matrix to yield a matrix of rational scores. Then this matrix is multiplied by another weighting matrix, to yield a matrix of estimated criterion scores. This procedure gives the same estimated criterion scores that would result if we first obtained the product of the weighting matrix for the rational scores by the weighting matrix for the criterion scores and then multiplied the data matrix of scores by this product matrix. The proof of this is given at the end of this chapter.

The rational scale approach implies an overall set of personality dimensions that includes all the socially significant aspects of human personality. If, in fact, one has formulated a set of labels that does include most of these dimensions, and if one has developed sets of items, responses to which do reflect these dimensions, then by definition one has assembled a set of items which should enable him to sample most of the important types of behaviors for socially significant criterion variables. Obviously, the construction of a multiscale instrument to predict success in each of most of the socially significant activities of a collective society is merely an ideal to be striven for. Nevertheless, to have this as a model can be useful for the development of rational, criterion, or factor scales.

BACKGROUND FOR FACTOR SCALES

We saw in Chapter 3 that factor analysis provides a basis for determining objectively, for any specified set of items or other variables, the number of distinct dimensions represented in the set. More specifically, for a given number of factors we can determine what percentage of the variance of the data matrix can be accounted for. Procedures are available for calculating both a matrix of factor scores from the original data matrix and a factor loading matrix that can be used as a weighting matrix for reproducing each of the observed variables from the factor scores. However, the factor analytic procedures can give us no more information than is latent in the data matrix on a particular group of individuals and a particular set of variables or items.

It is useful, though not essential, to have some hypothesis as to the total number of independent dimensions in the domain to be investigated. For example, if one wishes to construct a multiple factor scale instrument for measuring the dimensions of personality, a priori hypotheses concerning the number of dimensions within the personality domain can be useful. The "needs" of Murray (1938) provide such a set of hypotheses. Edwards (1953) used these "needs" as a basis for selecting a set of fifteen hypothesized dimensions for which he constructed items and which resulted in the Edwards Personal Preference Schedule. Because of the forced choice format of this instrument, the scores are ipsative. Therefore the number of dimensions of the multiscale cannot exceed one less than the number of scales. This is proved at the end of this chapter. The properties of ipsative scales in general are discussed by Clemans (1966). The use of multiple sets of scores yielded by such ipsative scales requires special statistical procedures. These have been used by Karr (1958) in a study of the Edwards items. The Edwards Personal Preference Schedule assumes a dimensionality of fifteen which is reduced to fourteen by the mathematical artifact of ipsatization.

The work of Edwards (1957) illustrates the utility of the rational approach. As might be expected, the rational approach can result in redundancy. An analysis by Wright (1957) on the individual items of the Edwards scale yielded nine or ten factors. Another study based on Murray's rational dimensions was made by Campbell (1959). She used twenty-four of his hypothesized dimensions and constructed twelve items from each. Again, factor analysis revealed only ten to twelve factors. Nevertheless, in spite of these redundancies Murray's rational approach has provided a useful foundation for the development of factor scales.

CRITERION SCALES

In rational scales a set of dimensions or attributes is hypothesized, whereas in criterion scales a set of variables established by others is specified. One of the criterion scale approaches attempts to segregate items that can be scored so as best to estimate a person's success in or conformity to each criterion activity. Criterion scales have sometimes been referred to as group discriminative scales, but such a designation implies only a very special type of multiple criterion scales. We shall develop the more general model based on multiple criteria and show that the conventional procedure for constructing multiple criterion personality scales is a special case. The more general model has been discussed by the author (Horst, 1954, 1955) in previous publications. Here we shall give only a summary review of the general model and examine its implications for the special case of measurement of personality dimensions. We shall discuss the criterion variables, the predictor variables, the predictor set, the weighting or scoring vectors, and the role of criterion variables for psychological measurement in general.

CRITERION VARIABLES

In multiple regression statistics, criterion variables have traditionally been called dependent variables. Criterion variables are usually those of considerable social significance, such as success in jobs, marriage, and school. In general, it may take a long time to find out how successful one is in the criterion activity. The cost of obtaining this information may also be of considerable magnitude. For example, the criterion of the professional category "lawyer" may be income at some given age, but it will take much time and money to learn how successful a youth of twenty will be in terms of income at the age of forty if he trains to be a lawyer.

The concept of multiple criterion scales assumes that in a number of areas of activity of social significance where rewards and penalties are meted out, success might be predicted from personality type items. This is only a special case of the more general case where success in a large number of different kinds of activities may be predicted. An example of prediction in another type of activity is a testing program in the state of Washington. Here high school seniors who plan to enter institutions of higher learning in the state are required to take a battery of tests. Scores on these tests, together with grade point averages in various high school subject areas, are used to predict success in each of approximately forty different college course academic areas, as a basis for helping the student choose his areas of specialization.

The number of criterion variables one might wish to have represented in his multiple scale, and the specific criteria included, may vary widely from one enterprise to another. Usually, however, they will be limited to a set of occupations or professions, academic course areas, types of mental abnormalities, or military occupational specialties.

In one common method of constructing criterion scales, the scores in the criterion data matrix are generated by what is called the group discriminative strategy. Here one is not concerned with degree of adjustment or success in a particular criterion category but only with whether a person belongs to that category. For example, if the attributes are professional designations, such as lawyer, engineer, or teacher, then a person's criterion value for a lawyer would be 1 if he is a lawyer and 0 if not. For each criterion category we have a binary designation for inclusion or exclusion from the category in question. Such procedures for indicating membership give no information about degrees of success within the group activity. The implication of this procedure is that in general those who belong to the group tend to have more ability with respect to the activities required by that group than those who do not belong to the group. Perhaps a case may be made for this assumption for group categories in general, but its validity has not been clearly demonstrated.

The problems of multiple criteria in general, of which the multiple criterion scale is a special case, are complicated. Considerable methodological and empirical research is still required to obtain optimal results from the information which could realistically be obtained in life situations. In view of these problems, the multiple criterion scale approach has probably received more attention than is warranted.

PREDICTORS

In the general model of the multiple criterion set we may have several or more criterion or dependent variables and also a set of predictor variables. These predictor variables may be psychological tests, physiological variables, environmental variables, or whatever we choose. It is not even necessary that we restrict the concept of criterion and predictor variables to the discipline of psychology or the social sciences. The concepts of predictor or independent variables and criterion or dependent variables are well known in classical multiple regression analysis. In general, the predictor variables are those from which the criterion variables are estimated or predicted. In contrast to the criterion variables, they are typically easily and cheaply assessed for a group of individuals. Furthermore, the reactions or assessments with reference to the predictor variables are of no particular interest as such; they are of interest only as they can be used to estimate values on variables that provide the basis for rewards and penalties.

The multiple criterion type of personality instrument is not concerned with the dimensions of personality. Usually there is no interest in theoretical considerations of personality structure as such. From the multiple prediction point of view, each item in the multiple criterion personality scale may be regarded as a separate variable. The problem is to determine how responses shall be quantified for these sets of stimulus elements or statements so as to yield estimates of the criterion variables, whether they be estimates of success, adjustment, group inclusion, or some other variable.

PREDICTION SET

We see then that the multiple criterion scale model for personality measurement is a special case of the general model which includes both predictor and criterion variables. This model assumes errors of measurement in the criterion variables but not in the predictors. The predictor variables are sometimes referred to as fixed variables and the criterion variables as random variables. We shall consider several different types of multiple prediction sets.

In the first and simplest case, we have one predictor variable and one criterion variable. For example, we may have a single item in a personality scale and a single criterion variable of success as a machinist. The item might be, "I like to work with tools." Responses on this item may correlate high with measures of success as a machinist. One may then use the item to help predict success as a machinist.

In a second type of multiple prediction set, we have a number of predictors and a single criterion. For many criterion variables one can do a better job of prediction with a number of different predictor variables, provided they satisfy certain well-known statistical requirements, than with a single predictor variable.

We may also have one independent variable and a number of dependent or criterion variables. The predictor variable may be a score obtained from an instrument designed to measure general intelligence as a unidimensional trait. Scores from such tests have been used extensively to predict success in a large number of different criterion areas, including academic, vocational, and military. This model does not enable one to determine in which of a number of different criterion areas one might be most successful. Differential prediction is not possible from a single predictor variable. In the single scale model discussed in Chapter 3, this single predictor is precisely the model implied. If a group of items has been assembled with the assumption that the set measures only a single function, it may not logically be used for such purposes as prediction, estimation, diagnosis, or prognosis, where a number of different criterion variables are implied unless these variables are assumed to be highly correlated.

The most general type of multiple prediction model includes both multiple predictor and multiple criterion variables. This is the paradigm for scales which purport to estimate a number of different criterion variables. The Strong Vocational Interest Blank (1943), for example, was designed to be scored in a number of different ways to yield estimates on a large number of occupational and professional criterion variables. The multiple criterion and predictor model is the optimal prediction model for most institutional prediction programs, but its use in various institutional segments of our society has been limited.

WEIGHTING OR SCORING VECTORS

Given a set of personality items and a set of criterion variables, such as a number of groups or life activities, procedures are available for estimating from responses to the personality items the criterion values for each of the criterion variables for the persons who took the test. In Chapter 1, we discussed at some length problems and procedures involved in the quantification of responses to the stimulus elements in a psychological or personality measuring instrument. For each person responding to the set of stimulus elements, there is a vector of binary numbers in the data matrix. For each possible response, there is either a 1 or a 0, depending on whether the examinee did or did not respond to that element. There are also vectors of ideal weights, determined in some fashion, of the same order as the response vector. The score from each scoring vector is the sum of the ideal weights corresponding to the unit elements in the subject's response vector. More simply, a person's score is the minor product of his response vector and the ideal vector. For criterion scales there is a scoring vector corresponding to each criterion.

APPROXIMATE SOLUTIONS FOR SCORING VECTORS

We shall now consider in more detail methods for obtaining scoring vectors for criterion type personality scales. Hase and Goldberg (1966) describe the procedure as follows: "In constructing an inventory by the empirical group discriminative (or criterion group) strategy, the test constructor initially attempts to locate two distinct groups of subjects who differ in some significant manner, for example, psychotics versus normals, lawyers versus men in general, males versus females, or who fall at each pole of a personality trait he seeks to measure. The test items are then administered to members of both criterion groups. Differences in the responses of these groups to each item are examined and those items discriminating between the groups at a desired level of significance are retained for a scale. Only the empirically determined, discriminating power of the item determines item selection for a scale and the scale is particularly labeled in terms of the criterion groups utilized. Most of the standard scales of the MMPI and the CPI were constructed by the group discriminative strategy."

The quotation suggests that one of the criterion measures can be a personality trait which the investigator seeks to measure. It should be noted, however, that here the criterion personality trait is one that has been hypothesized and therefore is a rational rather than an empirical variable. The question of how one gets measures of people on this criterion personality trait in order to divide them into high and low groups must be answered. The implication is that one has another personality scale of some kind that is used to measure the criterion variable. The procedure implies that one group of personality items is available as a criterion measure for validating or developing a scale to measure the same thing from another group of personality items.

Another aspect of the procedure indicated by the quotation is the division of the total group into subgroups, such as psychotic versus normals, lawyers versus men in general, and so on. This yields the binary criterion data matrix in which the 1's and 0's represent group membership or exclusion respectively. Such a criterion set, with its dichotomous metric for the experimental group, is a special case of the multiple prediction–multiple criterion model. The predictor data submatrix may be a binary matrix having 0's for elements not responded to and 1's for those elements that have been responded to. If degrees of agreement are permitted, then one may arbitrarily assign integer weights to the response elements. The score is the integer corresponding to the response element marked.

In the approach suggested by Hase and Goldberg, one obtains a criterion binary data matrix whose elements correspond to group membership criteria. The more general criterion data matrix, where degrees of adjustment are implied for each of the criterion variables, introduces theoretical and computational problems. Empty cells will occur because all persons do not engage in all of the criterion activities. Let us assume, however, that the criterion submatrix has no unknown elements in it, just as in the case of the group membership criterion discussed by Hase and Goldberg.

Beginning with such a data matrix with its criterion and predictor submatrices, Hase and Goldberg then discussed the conventional procedure of using the criterion vectors as a basis for getting group discrimination indices for each of the predictor or personality items. One may segregate subsets of items showing the highest degree of relationship with the various criteria. Presumably the score on each subset or scale is the number of items marked according to the key determined by the analyses. If graded responses are provided, then the procedures for item selection and item scoring are a little more involved, but no difficult problems are encountered.

This approach to the development of a multiple criterion personality scale is an approximation to the classical methods. With these more precise methods one simply calculates a multiple regression matrix of weights based on the data matrix of predictor and criterion measures. This procedure is straightforward and is outlined at the end of this chapter.

ASSUMPTIONS IN APPROXIMATE WEIGHTING METHODS

As pointed out by Hase and Goldberg, the group discrimination method has been used extensively in the construction of criterion scales. Let us see now what approximations to the optimal least square procedure are implied by the conventional group discrimination method. The traditional least square procedure gives the "best" estimates of the criterion for the sample. Then if the multiple regression matrix is postmultiplied into the data matrix to give an estimate of the criterion matrix, the sum of the squares of the discrepancies between the estimated and observed criterion elements will be as small as or smaller than that yielded by any other method. This procedure takes into account not only the relationships of the predictor variables with the criterion variables but also the intercorrelations of the predictor variables among themselves. It is irrelevant whether we have group discrimination or discrete criterion variables. It can be readily shown that discrimination functions are special cases of least square estimates where the criterion variables are dichotomous.

The first assumption made by the conventional group differentiation method is that the intercorrelations among the predictor variables are zero. This is, for all practical purposes, never the case and sometimes not sufficiently approximated to justify procedures based on the assumption. Second, there is the assumption that one knows what are high and what are low values. Conventional tests of significance are well known to be arbitrary with reference to the confidence interval chosen, therefore they are of limited value for deciding which items discriminate and which do not. But let us assume that the researcher does have some more or less satisfactory way of deciding which items discriminate adequately for each of the criterion groups. He may then cluster these into subsets and assume that the intercorrelations among the predictor variables are zero, that the selected items have regression weights which do not differ significantly from one another, and that the unselected items have weights which do not differ significantly from zero. By this time, we may have compounded a series of questionable assumptions.

An extensive body of methodology and rationale exists for handling a multiple predictor and criterion set of observations so as to give maximum differential prediction among any specified set of criteria. One reason such procedures have not been more generally used is that much more computational labor is required than for the cruder methods. However, with the general availability of electronic computer facilities, this should not be a serious deterrent.

ALLOCATIONS OF ITEMS TO SCALES

Even if the traditional group discrimination approximation to the optimal multiple regressional approach is employed for multiple criterion scales, there are several possibilities for unit scoring. By means of covariance or other discrimination indices, one may select items for subscales within the larger pool for each of the criterion variables. However, one must decide whether the subsets are to be mutually exclusive or whether an item may appear in more than one of the subsets. Either strategy of item selection poses problems. In a set of item discrimination indices, it is usually not clear what the unique assignment of an item should be. This aspect of subset grouping of items is a special case of the optimal classification problem that has been discussed by Dwyer (1954), Votaw (1952), Lord (1952), Brogden (1946), Thorndike (1950), Horst (1960), and Sorenson (1965). There are various ways in which one may assign items to single categories so that the overall sum of the item discrimination indices is a maximum. One may allocate items in such a way that the overall average of allocated indices is a maximum for all criterion categories. But the average for the category having the highest average may be very much greater than for the one having the lowest average. Further constraints may be put on strategies of allocation so that the variance of the averages of the indices for the various criterion categories is minimized.

Even if one has resolved this problem, there is a further question as to the number of items assigned to each of the categories. For example, we may require that an approximately equal number of items be allocated to each category. Such a constraint may impose further restrictions on the variation of average item indices for the range of criterion categories. It may be possible to assign an equal number to each category in such a way that the overall average will be a maximum, and so that the variation in averages over the range of categories will be acceptably small.

If one has some rational or empirical order of preference for the categories, he can begin with the most important. Having determined the number of items to be assigned to each category, he can assign the items with the highest indices on the first category to it. The specified number of remaining items with the highest item indices for the next category may be assigned to it, and so on until all items have been assigned. The obvious difficulty with such a procedure is that the items assigned to the last category will almost certainly have much lower indices for that category than those assigned to the preceding categories will have for their respective categories.

There is, of course, the possibility that items can be placed in more than one category and this relaxation will make the assignment of items much easier. As we already know, multiple category assignment of items can result in high intercorrelations of criterion scale scores and thus reduce criterion differentiation. One can, however, use both positive and negative scoring for the items as indicated by the item indices. Some of the items may be positively keyed for one category and negatively for another. Such reversals will tend to result in lower intercorrelations among the scale scores and justify multiple allocation of items. However, this strategy of multiple role item selection and scoring implies a modification of the counting operation for the various scale scores. Scoring keys can be devised to maintain the additive counting procedure so that an item will be correct if marked positively in one scale and negatively in another. This scoring strategy preserves the simple counting operation without the introduction of positive and negative numbers.

MULTIPLE REGRESSION APPROACH

The generalized multiple regression approach for multiple prediction sets encounters difficulty with degrees of freedom when the number of variables is very large compared to the number of cases. This would most surely be the case with personality scales where each item is regarded as a separate variable and where the number of items may be large, such as 400 or 500. For these cases, the generalized optimal multiple prediction model cannot be used. An approach to the solution for such problems was developed by the author (Horst, 1941). More recently, applications of the procedure have been made by Leiman (1951), Burket (1964), and Roudabush (1963). As a matter of fact, it is probable that this more generalized approach should supplant the traditional multiple regression approach. The more general approach assumes errors in both the predictor and criterion variables. Errors of measurement do occur in predictor measures. In many psychological measures, errors are doubtless as prevalent in predictor measures as in criterion measures.

GENERAL ROLE OF CRITERION VARIABLES IN PSYCHOLOGY

It is probable that any psychological enterprise must be evaluated, in the last analysis, in terms of its contributions to the welfare of a collective society. This observation extends beyond the realm of scientific discipline. We cannot escape a consideration of the role of human values in psychological research, and in other disciplines as well. Criterion variables imply concepts about what is good or bad in a collective society. We may well question, then, whether the concept of multiple criterion personality scales is a useful or appropriate model, if one is primarily concerned with the measurement of the dimensions of personality. In such an enterprise, one would presumably be interested primarily in the prediction of socially significant criterion variables. But whether these variables, as such, appropriately enter into the development of multiple scale personality instruments in a direct fashion is doubtful. The alternative procedure will be considered in the next section.

FACTOR SCALES

We have seen that factor analytic procedures enable us to obtain a useful estimate of the dimensionality of a set of variables measured on a given sample of individuals. We have also seen that by appropriate computational and mathematical procedures, they enable us to establish a set of dimensions which appeal to common sense or to psychological sense. We have discussed the rational and the criterion scale approaches to personality measurement and have indicated some of the objections to these approaches. We have seen that the rational scale approach may be useful as a basis for the factor analytic approach.

Some criticisms of the factor techniques are that the results are often confusing and conflict with those of other investigators. These weaknesses are alleged to contradict the claims of the factor analysts that the techniques do yield results that make psychological sense. It is possible, of course, to misuse any technique, methodology, or procedure. Furthermore, although theoretically the factor analytic approach may be the best, there is still not complete agreement as to what are the best factoring techniques. In *Factor Analysis of Data Matrices* (Horst, 1965), many of the techniques and underlying rationales of factor analysis are presented. The alternatives to factor analysis, namely, the criterion scales, the rational scales, and (if one wants to include them) the single and the random scales, are even more subject to criticism.

An issue that has confused factor analytic models and procedures concerns the different types of factors discussed in Chapter 3—the specific, common, and general factors. Many investigators have been concerned with the reality of these various types of factors and have not recognized that they are consequences of the particular factor analytic procedures used. One can find or fail to find general factors according to whether or not he includes them in his basic model. This is also the case with specific factors. One frequently reads in the literature that a general factor was found. This merely indicates that the investigator used a computational procedure that encouraged such a factor to appear. The issue of communality, which we shall discuss in more detail later, also involves model construction rather than the verification or denial of hypotheses.

An unfortunate result of the proliferation of factor analytic studies is the vast number of factors which has been dredged up. One may have hypotheses as to the total number of factors within a psychological domain. If this number is very large, he can certainly design studies and use techniques to produce a large number of factors. On the other hand, it is possible to design studies to find the minimum number of factors required to account adequately for the systematic variation in a set of observations. The evidence to date in the personality area is that this number most likely will not exceed twenty or twenty-five. As a matter of fact, most of the competent factor analytic studies that have been conducted on personality type items and scales have not yielded more than ten or twelve clear-cut factor dimensions.

Factor scales may be constituted in a number of different ways. One method segregates mutually exclusive subsets of items, another segregates overlapping subsets. Both of these procedures are also used for rational and criterion scales. A third procedure results in what are called primary factor scores.

MUTUALLY EXCLUSIVE SUBSETS OF ITEMS

A factor analysis gives a factor loading matrix that indicates the extent to which each of the variables or items is saturated with a particular factor, assuming that we have applied a simple structure transformation. We find from the factor loading matrix which variables have the highest loading in each factor. These factor loadings may provide the basis for segregating mutually exclusive subsets of items. In the next chapter we shall consider in more detail the criteria that can be used in the allocation of items to scales, and some of the limitations of this use of factor loadings for constructing factor scales.

OVERLAPPING ITEM GROUPS

With factor scales, as with criterion and rational scales, it is possible to assign an item to more than one scale. Also, one can reverse the direction or polarity of two-choice items. The strategies that call for grouping of items in the subscales assume that the items are dichotomously scored as right or wrong. If this is the case, then with the overlapping strategy of item allocation, items may be keyed positively or negatively, depending on which group they are assigned to.

FACTOR SCORES

It is usually assumed that an adequate approximation to a data matrix may be expressed as a major product of a factor score matrix and the transpose of a factor loading matrix where the common order of the two matrices is much less than either the number of cases or the number of variables. This common order is, of course, the number of factors. The methods for grouping subsets of items, whether they be mutually exclusive or overlapping, should yield approximations to the factor score matrix. These grouping methods were used in the factor scales developed by Guilford (1959), Cattell (1957), and others. However, the simple grouping methods tend to give biased estimates of the mathematically more accurate factor scores that can be solved for by methods presented in later chapters. We shall see that the factor score matrix can be calculated by multiplying the data matrix by a matrix derived from the factor loading matrix. A crucial step in the development of factor scales is the calculation of this derived matrix and various modifications and simplifications of it.

It should be evident by now that the factor analytic models include both scaling and psychometric objectives. It is curious indeed that the work on scaling theory and methodology and that on psychometrics and psychological measurement have not recognized the integration of these two technologies in the factor analytic techniques. Thurstone, who led the way in the scaling techniques and made many contributions to psychological measurement theory and to factor analytic theory and methodology, did not explicitly recognize factor techniques as the synthesis of psychometrics and scaling theory. However, this is understandable since his chief interest in factor analysis was as an exploratory tool for determining the fundamental variables of a poorly structured discipline such as psychology.

MATHEMATICAL PROOFS

ITEM CRITERION WEIGHTS FROM RATIONAL SCALES

Let X be a matrix of binary item scores and B a binary item clustering matrix which groups items into rational scales. Let

$$W = XB \tag{4.1}$$

where W is now a matrix of rational scores. Let Y be a matrix of criterion scores. Consider

$$\epsilon = Y - WA \tag{4.2}$$

where A is determined so as to minimize some function of the ϵ_{ij}. In particular, this could be a least square solution. From Equation 4.1,

$$WA = XBA \tag{4.3}$$

If we let

$$\tilde{Y} = WA \tag{4.4}$$

$$G = BA \tag{4.5}$$

we may write

$$\tilde{Y} = XG \tag{4.6}$$

where $\tilde{Y}$ is the estimate of Y. Then we may calculate G directly from Equation 4.5. Since X is binary, we may calculate estimates of criterion scores directly from Equation 4.6 merely by summing elements in G, as indicated by the 1's in X, without first calculating rational scale scores.

REDUCED RANK OF IPSATIVE DEVIATION MEASURES

Let X be a vertical $N \times n$ matrix of ipsative measures. Then by definition,

$$X1 = c1 \tag{4.7}$$

where c is a scalar.

Consider the deviation matrix

$$Z = \left(I - \frac{1\,1'}{N}\right) X \tag{4.8}$$

where N is the height of X. From Equation 4.8

$$Z1 = X1 - \frac{1\,1'X1}{N} \tag{4.9}$$

From Equations 4.7 and 4.9

$$Z1 = c1 - \frac{1\,1'(c1)}{N} \tag{4.10}$$

or because the order of the unit vector is N, we have from Equation 4.10

$$Z1 = 0 \tag{4.11}$$

It can be proved (Horst, 1963) that the rank of the product of two matrices cannot be less than the sum of their ranks less their common order. We let t be the rank of Z and define the rank of a null matrix as zero. Then from Equation 4.8

$$0 \gtrless t + 1 - n \tag{4.12}$$

or

$$t \lessgtr n - 1 \tag{4.13}$$

Therefore the rank of Z cannot exceed $n - 1$.

THE GENERAL LEAST SQUARE SOLUTION FOR
ESTIMATING A MATRIX OF CRITERION MEASURES
FROM A MATRIX OF PREDICTOR MEASURES

We let

Z be an $N \times n$ matrix of standardized predictor measures,
Y be an $N \times m$ matrix of standardized criterion measures,
β be an $n \times m$ matrix of regression weights, and
ϵ be an $N \times m$ matrix of residuals.

Then

$$\epsilon = Y - Z\beta \tag{4.14}$$

The least square solution for β in Equation 4.14 minimizes the trace of $\epsilon'\epsilon$. It is well known that the solution for β is

$$\beta = (Z'Z)^{-1}Z'Y \tag{4.15}$$

If we let

r_{ZZ} be the matrix of correlations among the predictors and
r_{ZY} be the matrix of correlations of the predictors with the criteria,

then Equation 4.15 can be written

$$\beta = r_{ZZ}^{-1}r_{ZY} \tag{4.16}$$

If we let

D_σ be a diagonal matrix of the standard deviation of the predictors,
M be a vector of predictor means, and
X be the raw score matrix,

then

$$Z = (X - 1M')D_\sigma^{-1} \tag{4.17}$$

From Equation 4.17

$$Z\beta = (X - 1M')D_\sigma^{-1}\beta \tag{4.18}$$

We let

$$b = D_\sigma^{-1}\beta \tag{4.19}$$

$$M'D_\sigma^{-1}\beta = V' \tag{4.20}$$

$$Z\beta = \tilde{Y} \tag{4.21}$$

From Equations 4.18 through 4.21,

$$\tilde{Y} = [X,1]\begin{bmatrix} b \\ V' \end{bmatrix} \tag{4.22}$$

We let

$$_sX = (X,1) \tag{4.23}$$

$$B = \begin{bmatrix} b \\ V' \end{bmatrix} \tag{4.24}$$

From Equations 4.22 through 4.24

$$\tilde{Y} = {}_sXB \tag{4.25}$$

In particular, if X is a matrix of item scores, Equation 4.25 indicates the least square estimation of the criterion scores from the item scores and the scoring matrix B.

CHAPTER 5

Factor Scores

*I*n Chapter 4 we concluded that factor analysis provides the best available objective method for determining and measuring the dimensions of the personality domain as defined by a large pool of behavior items. In this chapter we shall consider in more detail the factor scores introduced in Chapter 4. Traditionally these scores have received much less attention from the factor analysts than has the factor loading matrix, but factor scores are of primary interest in the measurement of personality dimensions. We shall discuss kinds of factor scores, the grouping of items, least square methods, and integer scoring procedures.

KINDS OF FACTOR SCORES

We shall consider first the types of factor scores corresponding to the kinds of factor loadings previously discussed, and then briefly, the computational types which will be discussed in more detail in succeeding sections.

FACTOR SCORE TYPES

In Chapter 3 we described three kinds of factors that have been postulated in factor analysis models—common factors, general factors, and specific factors. By far the greatest interest has centered around the common factors. These are the factors which have loadings in several or more of the tests in a set. The method for calculating common factor loadings depends on the assumptions about specific and general factors.

It has been customary, whatever the kinds of factors postulated in the model, to calculate the factor loading matrix before calculating the factor score matrix. This is not necessary if one assumes no specific factors. As we have shown in *Factor Analysis of Data Matrices* (Horst, 1965), the obverse method of factor analysis calculates first the factor score matrix, then the factor loading matrix. The procedures and rationale developed in the following chapters are based on a factor model that does not use the concepts of specific and general factors. Reasons for the adoption of such a model are presented later in this chapter.

Interest in calculating specific factor scores corresponding to specific factor loadings has been less than that of calculating common factor scores. One reason is that a major objective of factor analysis has been to provide parsimonious descriptions of empirical variables. The number of common factors compared to the total number of variables is small, but by definition there are as many specific factors as there are variables. Therefore, if one were to calculate both common factor scores corresponding to the common factor loadings and specific factor scores corresponding to the specific factor loadings, the total number of factor measures would exceed that of the original measures by the number of common factors. Since there would be more factor scores than observed scores, profligacy rather than parsimony would result.

Nevertheless, the postulation of specific factors in a model does imply specific factor scores, and investigators have recognized the logical necessity of providing methods for the calculation of specific factor scores for this model. Two general types of methods have been proposed for their calculation. The first of these is based on the assertion that specific factor scores cannot be calculated but only estimated, and implies that linear combinations of the observed variables yield the specific factor scores. Common factor scores, too, are calculated as linear combinations of the observed variables. But these procedures for calculating both types of factor scores imply the product of the data matrix by a weighting matrix of some kind. It can readily be proved that such procedures for calculating specific and common factor scores must yield sets of scores that are not independent. This proof is given at the end of the chapter. Since the specific factor scores calculated in this way are not independent of common factor scores, they cannot properly be called "specific."

The other type of method for calculating specific factor scores has been set forth by Guttman (1955) and will not be elaborated upon in this book. This procedure does in fact yield specific factor scores which are uncorrelated or mutually orthogonal and which are also orthogonal to common factor scores. Such specific factor scores must be some function of a matrix which is orthogonal to the data matrix of test or item scores. Matrices orthogonal to the data matrix can be readily found, provided such a data matrix has at least twice as many entities as attributes and the original data matrix is basic. This basis for calculating specific factor scores, however, yields an infinite number of solutions. A unique mathematical definition for such specific factor scores has not yet been offered, although it should not be difficult to develop such a definition. While the mathematical and theoretical problems involved in the calculation of specific factor scores are interesting, the practical implications of such calculations have not been explored.

The third type of score is the general factor score. Schmid

and Leiman (1957) have developed a general model for higher order general factors. Methods for calculating higher order sets of general factors are based on oblique transformations of factor loading matrices. The general factors construct is closely associated with the concepts of oblique transformations and specific factors. These relationships are discussed in some detail in Chapter 10 of *Factor Analysis of Data Matrices* (Horst, 1965). As indicated in Chapter 4, general factors appear or fail to appear only as they are incorporated into the model or excluded from it.

If one wishes to include the concept of general factors, the model of higher order general factors developed by Thurstone (1947) appears to provide the most sophisticated mathematical definition available for general factors. Only by calculating second order general factor loadings can first order general factor loadings be adequately defined and calculated. The rationale and procedures for doing this are discussed in *Factor Analysis of Data Matrices* (Horst, 1965). There it is also pointed out that second order common factors reappear as first order general factors and that second order specific factors correspond to first order common factors. The rationale and computational procedure for first order general factor scores is also given in *Factor Analysis of Data Matrices*.

It is generally assumed that factors from oblique transformations can be more readily interpreted than those from orthogonal transformations. If oblique transformations are used, then, in order to reproduce the correlation matrix from the factor loading matrix, the general as well as the common factor loadings are required. It has not been generally recognized, however, that oblique transformations can yield imaginary as well as real general factors. This has been noted by Johnson (1957).

The concept of general factors has important implications for stability of factor loadings from one sample to another. Either one must assume that the transformation matrix characterizes the particular group to which it is applied and therefore varies from one sample to another, or that it reflects a more basic phenomenon with respect to the general factor. One cannot hypothesize invariant general factors and also attribute the correlations among the simple structure factor scores to variation among samples of persons. The mathematical justification for these statements is straightforward but somewhat involved and will not be further elaborated here.

COMPUTATIONAL TYPES

The most common computational procedure, when factor scales are used for multidimentional personality measurement, is based on the segregation of subsets of items. A more sophisticated approach is based on a least square solution for the factor score matrix.

Irrespective of whether a simple grouping of items is implied for each of the scales or whether the factor score matrix is calculated by least square methods, a practical consideration is the scoring of answer sheets. The most obvious method of simplification is the use of integer scoring vectors. A number of ways for using integer weights are available. The particular variation used depends largely on the degree of accuracy required. Some of the grouping methods may be regarded as special cases of integer scoring.

GROUPING OF ITEMS

Simple procedures that involve the segregation of subsets of items so that each of the separate subsets represents a particular factor dimension are particularly appealing. Since item grouping is the most common method of calculating factor scores, we shall discuss some of the important considerations involved in the procedure. We shall review the grouping methods, discuss some of the criteria for grouping, examine the bias of regression effects, and consider advantages of uncorrelated factor scores.

METHODS OF GROUPING

The essential characteristic of a grouping method is that a decision is required as to whether or not an item belongs to a particular factor dimension. If the grouping procedure is adopted, two alternatives are available. The item can be assigned to only one of the factor scales or it can be assigned to more than one. In the latter case, the direction of scoring for an item may vary from one group to another. The question of which is the high and which the low end of a set of response alternatives, whether they be binary or multiple, must be established with reference to each factor to which an item is assigned.

CRITERIA FOR GROUPING

One procedure for deciding to which factor scale an item should be allocated is based on the simple structure factor loading matrix. Ideally, this factor loading matrix is such that each factor has high loadings for only a relatively small number of variables and near zero loadings for all of the others. Ideally also, the direction of scoring for a variable or item should be such that the number of large negative loadings is minimized.

Some investigators, including Kaiser (1958), have recommended that before transformation procedures are applied to the arbitrary or principal axis factor loading matrix, the rows of the matrix should be normalized. Then each variable will carry an equal weight in determining the final transformed factor loading matrix. The assumption that each variable should carry an equal weight in this determination may be open to question. One may argue that those tests with higher communalities should have more weight than tests with lower communalities. A disadvantage to normalizing the principal axis factor loading matrix before transformation is that subsequent computations become more complicated. It is true, of course, that computational simplicity is not a necessary or sufficient criterion for computational and mathematical procedures, but other things being equal, the simpler methods are to be preferred.

After the transformation, whether or not normalization has taken place previously, one must still decide what to do about rescaling the row vectors of the transformed factor matrix. If they have been normalized prior to transformation and the transformation is square orthonormal, it is readily shown that the transformed matrix is still normal by rows. Then one may argue that the original communalities should be restored. The question of restoration is of course not encountered if the principal axis matrix was rotated without normalization. On the other hand, one can take the position that for easier interpretation of the test vectors, one should have normal test vectors in the simple structure matrix. The position we have adopted is that the influence of each test in the transformation should be a direct function of its communality, and therefore the tests with greater communalities will carry more weight than those with smaller ones. Thus it is neither necessary nor desirable to normalize the factor loading matrix before transformation.

We also adopt the position that the transformed or simple structure matrix should be obtained by a square orthonormal transformation, and thus we exclude the notion of general factors. Since the transformation is square orthonormal, the communalities of the transformed matrix will be the same as those in the basic structure or principal axis matrix. Thus the factor loading of a test for a given factor will reflect only that proportion of its total variance which is represented in that factor.

It has been traditional, following Thurstone, to list all variables which have factor loadings higher than .2 for a given factor in descending order of their factor loading for that factor. It is presumed that by a subjective study of the content of these variables, one can arrive at an acceptable label for the factor. There is nothing sacred about the .2 value; for purposes of labeling one may simply look at the names of the variables of those with highest loadings, using any point for cutoff he wishes.

One procedure for allocating items to a scale is to adopt some arbitrary point and say that all items with loadings higher than this shall be allocated to that factor scale. Depending on the number chosen, some overlapping will occur, resulting in multiple assignments.

It is not necessary that one use the same cutoff value for each factor. One may, for example, decide that each scale should include the same number of items. Thus, if there are 200 items and ten factors, one may decide that twenty items should be allocated to each factor. He would therefore identify the twenty items having the highest loadings in each factor, irrespective of how high these loadings are. He may not use all the items, but this procedure can result in the assignment of an item to more than one scale.

One may decide that items with no loadings higher than a given number, say .2, will be completely eliminated from the scales. One may also have other methods of eliminating items from further consideration. However, all procedures for eliminating items after the factor analysis has been completed assume that the factor saturations for the remaining items in the simple structure matrix would not have been much different if the eliminated items had been excluded from the set prior to the factor analysis. The validity of such assumptions depends on the number and characteristics of the items removed.

The methods of grouping we have suggested usually result in multiple assignments of items to scales. One method that does not result in multiple assignments allocates each item to the factor for which it has the highest loading. Although this procedure ensures that there will be no overlapping of items and that each item is allocated to a factor scale, there is no guarantee that items will be assigned to all of the factors. It is quite possible that for some of the factors no items will have their highest loading in that factor. Great variation in the number of items assigned to the factors can occur with this method. For example, with 200 items and ten factors, one factor may have fifty or more of the items with their highest loadings in it while others may have only eight, seven, or perhaps no more than one or two. If a factor has only one item with its highest loading in it, then by definition this would be a specific factor and the factor would be eliminated. One must, therefore, decide what is the minimum number of items that will be acceptable for a factor scale. Even six or seven items in a scale would probably not give a sufficiently reliable measure of the factor.

Therefore, the method of allocating items by columns of the factor loading matrix, while it can be made to yield the desired number of items in each factor, may result in many multiple assignments of items. Also, the unique assignments of items by rows may result in an uneven distribution of items assigned to the factors and in the elimination of one or more of the factors.

REGRESSION EFFECT OF ITEM GROUPING

One characteristic of the factor score matrices defined in Chapter 3 is that if orthonormal simple structure transformations are used, the resulting factor scores in the sample are uncorrelated. The methods outlined in later chapters approximate uncorrelated factor scores in the sample on which the analyses are performed. Empirical studies have shown that where item groupings have been made on the basis of the simple structure factor loading matrix, the correlations of the resulting factor scores tend to be significantly different from zero for many of the factor variables. Other things being equal, the more items two scales have in common, the higher will be the correlation between them.

It is possible, however, to include the same item in two scales but with reversed scoring, so that the correlations between the scales will be reduced. By having its sign reversed, an item can serve as a suppressor variable in a subset of items. The use of suppressor variables is discussed elsewhere at greater length by the author (Horst, 1941). However, even with the use of suppressor items, the grouping of items into scales may still result in significant correlations among the factor scores.

ADVANTAGES OF INDEPENDENT FACTOR SCORES

Grouping methods yield correlations among the factor scores which restrict their usefulness. Uncorrelated scores have definite advantages for prediction purposes. Such measures are more convenient than correlated measures for the predictor variables in multiple regression procedures. The multiple correlation of a set of uncorrelated independent variables with a criterion variable is the square root of the sum of squared zero order correlations of these independent variables with the criterion. Furthermore, the multiple regression coefficients are simply the zero order correlations of the orthogonal predictors with the criterion. The square of the zero order correlation may be interpreted as the percentage of variance common to two variables. Therefore we can determine at once, for any criterion variable, what proportion of its total variance each of the independent predictors accounts for. In general, of course, multiple regression coefficients from correlated variables cannot be interpreted in any simple fashion.

Even though item grouping methods yield correlated factor scores, it is possible to derive uncorrelated scores from item subset scales. One can determine empirically for a given sample the matrix of intercorrelations of factor scores based on item clustered subscales. From this correlation matrix one may find another matrix of weights which transforms the correlated factor scores to the best fitting uncorrelated factor scores. The procedures for doing this are indicated at the end of the chapter. In effect, these procedures use some of the factor variables to suppress the unwanted variance in a particular factor resulting from overlapping grouping methods.

LEAST SQUARE FACTOR SCORE METHODS

We have already indicated that by appropriate procedures we can obtain factor score matrices from a given sample of persons which do yield zero correlations among the factor scores. The mathematical details of this procedure are outlined elsewhere (Horst, 1966b). We shall in this section review the essential features of the least square orthonormal solution for the factor score matrix which does yield uncorrelated factor scores. This we shall do by considering in turn the arbitrary factor matrix, the simple structure factor matrix, the general inverse of the factor matrix, the sigma scaling of the general inverse, and scoring by a weighting matrix.

ARBITRARY FACTOR MATRIX

In Chapter 4 we showed that any data matrix may be approximated to any desired degree of accuracy by the major product* of a factor score matrix and a factor loading matrix. In the pro-

* Unless otherwise specified, the *major product* of two matrices is the product of a vertical matrix postmultiplied by a horizontal matrix, and the *minor product* is the product of a vertical matrix premultiplied by a horizontal matrix. (See Horst, 1963.)

cedures that follow, we assume that the exact solution, called the basic structure* or principal axis solution, is employed to obtain the original arbitrary factor loading matrix. We assume that acceptable criteria are available for determining the number of factors to be solved for, even though there is still considerable controversy as to how this number should be determined. In general, we solve for more basic structure factors than will probably be used in the final factor scale instrument. In the basic structure factor matrix the first factor accounts for the maximum possible amount of variance which a single factor can account for. The next factor accounts for the maximum possible amount of the remaining variance which an additional factor can account for, and so on. More generally, for a given number of basic structure or principal axis factors, the major product moment of the factor matrix reproduces the correlation matrix more accurately in the least square sense than any other product moment matrix of equal rank. Furthermore, the major product of this factor matrix by the corresponding optimal factor score matrix yields the best approximation in the least square sense to the data matrix. Most modern methods of factor analysis which use computers are based on the basic structure type of solution— more commonly known among mathematicians as an eigenvalue type solution.†

SIMPLE STRUCTURE FACTOR MATRIX

We have indicated that it is customary to transform the arbitrary or basic structure factor matrix to one which yields factors that are more easily interpreted. In this presentation we use the orthogonal rather than the oblique transformation. It is possible, as

---

* The *basic structure* of a real nonhorizontal matrix is defined as that triple product from left to right of a nonhorizontal orthonormal matrix by a diagonal matrix by a nonvertical orthonormal matrix which yields that real matrix. The diagonal elements of the diagonal matrix are all positive and in descending order of magnitude from upper left to lower right. (See Horst, 1963, 1965.)

† A special case of a basic structure solution is variously referred to by mathematicians as an *eigenvalue,* a *characteristic roots* and a *latent roots* solution.

indicated in *Factor Analysis of Data Matrices* (Horst, 1965), to calculate the simple structure matrix directly from either the correlation matrix or the normalized data matrix. However, the results are not in general precisely the same as if one applies the transformation to the principal axis factor matrix.

Having calculated the simple structure factor matrix by means of a square orthonormal transformation which satisfies Kaiser's varimax criterion (1958), we are ready to consider the calculation of the factor scores. At this point it is possible to apply some variation of the grouping methods and consider the job of multiple factor scale construction complete. This has been the procedure of some investigators who have used factor analytic techniques for constructing multiple factor scales for measuring personality. These are not, however, the mathematically optimal methods for solving for factor scores.

THE GENERAL INVERSE OF THE FACTOR LOADING MATRIX

The correct mathematical procedures for solving for the factor score matrices depend on the assumptions one has made about factor types. If one has assumed specific factors, the solution for the factor scores becomes more involved than if one does not assume them. If we are interested simply in getting the best approximation to the data matrix with the smallest number of factors, we should not postulate specific factors. This statement is neither an assumption, an opinion, nor a prejudice; it is merely a tautology. If one wishes to get the best approximation to the correlation matrix excluding the diagonal elements, this is quite another matter and one may advance many arguments for doing so. There is, however, no argument about the fact that specific factors are not permitted in minimum rank models for least square approximations to data matrices.

One may argue that this is not a good criterion, and that one should not attempt to account for the maximum variance in the data matrix with the minimum number of factors if such a procedure violates other objectives dear to the heart of the investigator.

If one admits specific factors, he concedes that the items he has chosen to measure the dimensions of personality may measure many dimensions that he is not interested in measuring or that are not worth measuring. If this is the case, the investigator should have chosen other items that do measure the dimensions of interest.

In any case, the model and the rationale we have adopted give a simple structure factor matrix that does not assume specific factors. We now require a procedure for obtaining optimal least square uncorrelated factor scores from this simple structure factor matrix. This means that we must solve for a weighting matrix having the same number of rows as there are variables or items and the same number of columns as there are factors, so that we can post-multiply the data matrix by it to get the matrix of uncorrelated factor scores. However, we need not actually calculate the factor score matrix. The solution for the weighting matrix and its proof are given elsewhere (Horst, 1966b). This solution is equivalent to the classical multiple regression type solution, but we use a more convenient concept known as the general inverse of a matrix.

The general inverse type solution does not appear to be well known among statisticians and mathematicians. It is surprising that their laborious and cumbersome traditional solutions have persisted so long. Procedures for solving for a system of linear equations, in which the number of unknowns and the number of equations is equal and in which the matrix of coefficients of the equations is basic, are well known. The solution of linear equations for other cases in which the number of equations and unknowns is not the same and in which the matrices of coefficients are not necessarily basic have traditionally not been treated as special cases of more general optimal solutions of linear equations. The more general solutions of which the exact solutions, the least square solutions, and nonbasic solutions are special cases, are set forth in Chapter 23 of *Matrix Algebra for Social Scientists* (Horst, 1963).

Having given the orthogonal simple structure factor loading matrix derived from the basic structure or principal axis factor loading matrix, it is a simple matter to express the general inverse of this matrix as a product involving the basic orthonormal, the basic diagonal, and the orthonormal transformation matrix. Such a formulation proves to be most convenient for computer programming.

SIGMA SCALING OF GENERAL INVERSE

The general inverse of the simple structure factor loading matrix is precisely the weighting matrix which, when postmultiplied into the normalized data matrix, yields the orthogonal factor score matrix for the sample. The major product of the factor score matrix by the simple structure factor loading matrix will yield the best approximation to the normalized data matrix in the least square sense. However, for most situations in which scoring procedures are to be applied to data matrices of response to items, the data matrix is not normalized and the general inverse of the simple structure matrix cannot be applied directly to the matrix of raw measures. The resulting factor scores will include certain constants that are functions of the means of the raw measures and of the scaled weighting elements. These factor scores can be readily converted to scores having equal means. The constants required for doing this may be incorporated as an augmented row of the weighting matrix. A corresponding column of unit elements is attached to the score matrix. The procedures and rationale for these operations are also discussed elsewhere (Horst, 1966b). For ease of interpretation, factor scores with means of 50 and standard deviations of 10 may be calculated. Such scores are known as T-scores.

SCORING BY WEIGHTING MATRIX

Scoring by means of the weighting matrix is readily accomplished by computers. One can store the weighting matrix in the computer either in core or on tape, and with a simple FORTRAN program read in the data cards for each person and compute his factor scores.

One may also use the general inverse weighting matrix as a basis for item grouping. This matrix enables one to identify suppressor items in subsets of variables. In general, the inverse solution will have many negative weights, which indicate the factors for which the item score is to be reversed. One still has to decide what strategy of item allocation to use, but for any particular strategy of item assignment one must be sure to reverse the direction of scoring for the items with negative weights in order that they may serve as suppressor variables.

INTEGER SCORING

We have seen that one may restrict scoring weights to 0 and 1. Obviously, in the item grouping methods the traditional scoring procedure has been to use only these weights. Scale scores are obtained by counting responses specified as correct for each item. This is a special case of the method of integer scoring where only two integers are provided, usually 0 and 1. We have also seen that the preferred method of obtaining factor scores from personality items is based on the use of a weighting matrix which is the general inverse of the simple structure factor matrix. This general inverse is rescaled by the reciprocals of the item standard deviations. Another alternative is available to us, however. The rescaled general inverse weighting matrix can be used as a basis for assigning integer weights to individual response elements. We shall discuss the number of response elements, the number of integers, the zero origin of integers, and scoring by response element integers.

NUMBER OF RESPONSE ELEMENTS

We shall assume that the number of response elements provided for each stimulus element is the same for all stimulus elements. We have indicated that the minimum number is two and that the maximum should not exceed nine or ten. Four or five response elements are probably optimal. The time and cost of integer scoring increases as the number of response elements increases.

We must distinguish between a response element that has a number associated with it and a response element that does not. In the cognitive type of response element set, where no scaling of the elements is assumed for the members of the set, we are not concerned about the assignment of scale values or numbers to each of the elements. However, for personality items with more than two responses, implied scale values are associated with each of the responses. We shall assume that the number of integers for the response alternatives is equal to the number of responses and that these proceed by successive integers such as 1, 2, 3, 4. This means that a person's score on an item is the integer assigned to the response he marked.

NUMBER OF INTEGERS IN THE SCORING MATRIX

Suppose now we consider procedures for scoring a data matrix, consisting of a limited range of integers such as from 1 to 5, with a set of numbers derived from the general inverse matrix scaled by the item standard deviations. A person's score for a particular factor would be the scalar product of his raw score vector and the vector of weights for that factor. Such a computational routine would be employed if factor scores were calculated by a computer.

We may, however, consider a simplified approach that could be carried out by hand for a limited number of cases in a relatively short time. Without loss of generality, we may take the lowest value for the integer assigned to a response as zero. Then by multiplying the highest weight in a particular factor weighting vector by the highest possible item score, one obtains the total possible range of product values which, when added together, yield a person's factor score. Instead of calculating such a score by a sum of products, the score might be the sum of successive integers from a set which goes from zero to some upper limit such as 5 or 8. One can therefore find a constant such that when the maximum possible product is divided by it, this number when truncated will yield the specified maximum integer. For a given scoring weight in the scoring vector corresponding to a particular test, there can be as many distinct products as there are response element scores, and each of these can be multiplied by the particular weight. These products can be divided by the constant determined on the basis of the maximum product and truncated. Thus for each factor and test, an integer weight may be determined for each of the response elements. This integer weight will lie somewhere between zero and the maximum integer decided upon for the set of integer scoring weights. In this way, one may determine a set of integers corresponding to each of the elements in a response set for each factor and each variable.

A person's factor score then will simply be the sum of the response weights for those elements he checked. By making the total number of integers in such a set sufficiently large, that is, by making the upper limit sufficiently high, one can approach a set of factor scores that are perfectly correlated with the mathematically exact factor scores. The smaller the highest integer permitted in the set of response weights, the less accurate will be the estimate of the precise factor scores. We have then a rationale and an operational procedure for obtaining by integer addition approximations to the scores that would be yielded by the more precise matrix multiplication procedures.

If one wishes to score answer sheets by hand, one can make up as many different scoring stencils as there are different scoring integers. For each different scoring integer, any one response element that is assigned that integer product weight for a given factor will have a corresponding opening in the stencil. One can simply count the number of times for each factor that a person responds to elements corresponding to each of the integers. If, for example, only five scoring weights have been allowed, then one will have five scoring stencils for each factor and get a count for each of the five integers from each of the five scoring stencils. One will then multiply the frequencies by the corresponding scoring weights to get the total score for the factor. In the limiting case, if the range of weights included only 0 and 1, then one would not score zero-weighted response elements, but count only the number of the unit-weighted response elements marked. This would constitute a special case of the item grouping method of scoring which has been traditional in factor scales and other multiscale types of personality measures.

ZERO ORIGIN OF INTEGERS

We indicated in the previous paragraph that the score value for the lowest response element may be arbitrarily taken as zero; then the higher weights would increase by increments of one. This means that the lowest scoring weight would also be zero. However, the method of establishing the scoring matrix described in the previous section can yield both positive and negative weights. Where negative weights occur in the general inverse of the factor score matrix, the direction of scoring of the item for the factor must be reversed. For such cases it is therefore necessary, in establishing the final weighting integers, to subtract each of the scoring integers from the maximum value to arrive at a set of reversed scoring weights.

For computational economy in calculating the factor scores, it is important to have zero origin for the scoring weights. Whether these calculations are made by computers or by hand scoring stencils, the assignment of zero to the extreme of the response weights means that this response is not considered in the scoring of the items. It gets a weight of zero, no matter what number it is multiplied by. Therefore, in the case of two-elements response sets one considers only one of the responses, namely, the one whose integer weight is unity.

SCORING BY RESPONSE ELEMENT WEIGHTS

The foregoing discussion has implied the computational procedures for arriving at factor scores by means of the summation of integers with any desired degree of approximation to the mathematically exact factor scores. In Chapter 10 we shall see that as the number of integer weights is increased, the resulting factor scores become more nearly orthogonal. If the number of weighting integers is sufficiently small, it is possible for some items to have zero weights for all response elements for all factors. This means that those items are eliminated from the set. Such results can occur if both the maximum absolute value in a row of the scaled general inverse matrix and the maximum value in the integer scoring vector are sufficiently low.

The rationales and procedures discussed in this section allow for the special case of the two-response element item and include both differential and unit weighting of the items in a scale. This procedure for integer scoring weights, therefore, can be used not only as a method for grouping items to be scored by simple counting of responses to keyed answers but also for differential weighting of these responses. Special cases of the method yield both unique and overlapping subsets. For either or both of these cases, suppressor items for the subsets can occur by means of the reversed scoring mechanisms, if these suppressor items have large enough negative weights to survive in the integering and truncating procedures. Mathematical and computer procedures for the integer response weight scoring methods have been developed (Horst, 1966b).

MATHEMATICAL PROOFS

CORRELATIONS BETWEEN COMMON AND SPECIFIC FACTORS EXPRESSED AS LINEAR FUNCTIONS OF OBSERVED SCORES

Let

Z be a $N \times n$ matrix of normalized observed scores where $N > n$,

Y_c be an $N \times t$ matrix of common factor scores where $n > t$, and

Y_s be an $N \times n$ matrix of specific factor scores.

Assume without loss of generality that

$$Y_c'Y_c = I \tag{5.1}$$

$$Y_s'Y_s = I \tag{5.2}$$

Let

$$Y_c = Zb_c \tag{5.3}$$

$$Y_s = Zb_x \tag{5.4}$$

Let the basic structure of Z be

$$Z = P\Delta Q' \tag{5.5}$$

From Equations 5.1 through 5.5 we may write

$$Y_c + Ph_c \tag{5.6}$$

$$Y_s = Ph_s \tag{5.7}$$

where h_c and h_s are orthonormal. The matrix of correlations r_{cs} between the common and specific factor scores, because of Equations 5.1 and 5.2, is

$$r_{cs} = Y_c'Y_s \tag{5.8}$$

Substituting Equations 5.6 and 5.7 in Equation 5.8 gives

$$r_{cs} = h_c'h_s \tag{5.9}$$

Since h_s is square orthonormal by definition, no orthonormal matrix exists which is orthogonal to it, hence r_{cs} cannot vanish.

THE BEST FITTING ORTHOGONAL FACTOR SCORE MATRIX FOR A NONORTHOGONAL FACTOR SCORE MATRIX

Let

Y be an $N \times t$ normalized matrix of correlated factor scores, and

W be the best fitting orthogonal matrix of factor scores.

Consider

$$W - Y = \epsilon \tag{5.10}$$

where

$$\operatorname{tr} \epsilon'\epsilon = \min \tag{5.11}$$

and

$$W'W = I \tag{5.12}$$

Let

$$U = \operatorname{tr}(\epsilon'\epsilon - W'W\lambda) \tag{5.13}$$

where λ is a symmetric matrix of Lagrangian multipliers. From Equations 5.10 and 5.13

$$\psi = \operatorname{tr}(W'W - 2W'Y + Y'Y - W'W\lambda) \tag{5.14}$$

Differentiating Equation 5.14 symbolically with respect to W' and equating to zero, we get

$$W - Y - W\lambda = 0 \tag{5.15}$$

or

$$W(I - \lambda) = Y$$

or

$$Y(I - \lambda)^{-1} = W \tag{5.16}$$

Because of Equation 5.12 and since λ is symmetric, we must have

$$(I - \lambda)^{-1} = (Y'Y)^{-\frac{1}{2}} \tag{5.17}$$

Let

$$r_{cc} = Y'Y = Q\Delta^2 Q' \tag{5.18}$$

From Equations 5.17 and 5.18

$$YQ\Delta^{-1}Q' = W \tag{5.19}$$

Therefore the best fitting orthogonal factor score matrix to Y is given by the transformation $Q\Delta^{-1}Q'$ which may be calculated from Equation 5.18.

CHAPTER 6

Psychological Issues

7 n this chapter we shall take up several psychological issues that are particularly relevant to the measurement of personality dimensions. We shall discuss these under the topics of social desirability, faking of responses, and scaling theory and psychometrics.

SOCIAL DESIRABILITY

In this section we shall examine several of the more strictly computational and operational concepts associated with the social desirability variable. These we shall discuss in terms of scaling for social desirability; scoring for social desirability; social desirability as a first principal axis; social desirability and item means; and correlations between social desirability scale values, item means, and principal axis factor loadings.

SCALING FOR SOCIAL DESIRABILITY

A number of different methods for scaling a series of stimulus situations give values that are highly correlated. Edwards (1964) and others have shown that, irrespective of the experimental groups who do the scaling, social desirability scale values come out about the same.

Earlier, one of Thurstone's (1929) objectives in the development of scaling techniques was the determination of an attitude score for a person by a summation of the scale values of the items he endorsed. The scaling of a set of items on the same group of individuals for which attitude scores were desired occurred somewhat later. Richardson (1933) formulated a rationale for getting both scale values for items and scale scores for persons from a set of items administered to only one group of individuals. His rationale was as follows: A person's attitude score should be the average of the scale values of the items he endorses, and the scale value of an item should be the average of the scores of persons who endorse that item. A slight modification of this formulation, including certain specifications about metric, was required to make the problem soluble.

SCORING FOR SOCIAL DESIRABILITY

If a group of subjects is asked to respond to a set of items in what they regard as the socially desirable manner, we get a data matrix. From this matrix we can obtain a factor loading vector that may be taken to represent the scale value for the social desirability variable. We can also obtain the corresponding factor score vector which may be regarded as a measure of the ability to recognize socially desirable responses for the individuals doing the rating. There are, however, simpler methods for obtaining social desirability scores. We can administer to a group of individuals a scale consisting of items with high social desirability values. A person's score may be taken as the number of items he endorses. Such scores tend to correlate high with scores on many personality scales alleged to measure different dimensions of personality.

There are individual differences in the ability to recognize what, according to some consensus, are socially desirable responses, and also in the tendency to give the socially desirable response. The failure to recognize the distinction between these two issues obscures the role that the social desirability factor plays in personality measurement. This factor has come to be regarded by some as something to be avoided or neutralized in personality measurement. Actually, it may well be that both the ability to recognize socially desirable behaviors and the tendency to conform to socially desirable mores are important components of personality dimensions.

These variables may be composites of more primary personality dimensions, just as the general intelligence factor as defined by McNemar (1964) and others may also be interpreted as a composite or principal axis for a number of more or less independent dimensions of intelligence. Perhaps the social desirability factor is a centroid for the social or interpersonal types of behavior as distinguished from the cognitive behaviors, just as the *G* factor is the centroid for cognitive types of activities.

SOCIAL DESIRABILITY AS FIRST PRINCIPAL AXIS

It may be that the concept of social desirability could be profitably investigated in terms of its analogy with intelligence. Suppose we administered to a group of students a large number of different tests, such as the ones Thurstone used in his primary mental abilities experiment (1938, 1941). Suppose that these tests include a wide variety of verbal, numerical, space relations, reasoning, and other material. Experience has shown that a factor analysis would yield high loadings for most such tests in the first principal axis. We might now score at random half of the tests in the reverse direction so that a high score would correspond to a small number of items correct and a low score to a high number of items correct. For example, the score of a person could be merely the total number of items in a test less the number of items answered correctly. It can readily be shown that in a factor analysis on a set of data in which half of the tests were scored in the reverse direction, the absolute values of the first principal axis factor loadings would be the same as for the original data; but for the tests with scoring reversed, the signs would be negative.

Suppose next that instead of providing the typical multiple choice alternatives for items of these tests, we proceed as follows: For each of the tests scored positively, the stem of each item would be followed by the statement, "Items of this kind are easy for me." For each of the tests scored negatively, the stem of each item would be followed by, "Items of this kind are difficult for me." The subjects would be required to give either a "yes" or a "no" response to each of the items. The score for each test would simply be the number of "yes" responses. Assume that all of the items are roughly at the 50 per cent level of difficulty for the group.

Suppose now one conducted a factor analysis on the scores obtained from this set of "personality" tests. Suppose that the first principal axis had high loadings for all the tests accompanied by the statement that the items are easy, and high negative loadings for all tests accompanied by the statement that the items are difficult.

Suppose next that one scaled each item for its social desirability value. It is not unreasonable to assume that for items of the traditional cognitive type one would get positive scale values for the items associated with the "easy" statements and negative scale values for those associated with the "difficult" statement. If one correlated the scale values of the tests with the first principal axis factor loadings, one would not be greatly surprised to get a high positive correlation.

Suppose next that we plotted the average scale values of the items in each of the "personality scales" with the first principal axis factor loadings of the original tests which had half of their directions reversed. Suppose also that we plotted the first principal axis factor loading of the "personality tests" with the corresponding first principal axis factor loadings of the cognitive tests for the sign reversal set. In general, let us assume that those tests having positive loadings in the cognitive set also have positive loadings in the "personality" set, and vice versa. Such results would not be surprising, nor would it be surprising to find high correlations among the scale values of the tests in the "personality" set. We might then conclude that the tendency to give socially desirable responses to the items was highly correlated with the tendency to give the correct responses. One might argue that persons do not reflect their true abilities in cognitive test items but that they give the socially desirable answers.

It is true that one would expect to find high correlations among the first principal axis factor loadings and the social desirability values of personality items. But the first principal axis is a hodgepodge, whether we are measuring personality dimensions, intelligence dimensions, or any other dimensions in any area of psychology or any other discipline. We should not attempt to interpret the first principal axis factor. To get meaningful results we should proceed with rotations to simple structure.

Suppose, however, that we did get a simple structure factor matrix from the principal axis factor matrix, and that for each of these factor loading vectors we calculated the correlations of the factor loadings with the corresponding social desirability scale values. Suppose we still found that there were appreciable correlations between the scale values and each of the simple structure factor loading vectors. One could argue that after going to all the trouble of doing a factor analysis on cognitive items, including the tricky operation of the simple structure transformation which presumably should make psychological sense, one still had not rid himself of the social desirability variable. If, however, we define the social desirability scale values of the cognitive tests as their first principal axis factor loadings, and calculate first principal axis factor scores, we need not go to all the trouble of performing an orthogonal simple structure transformation and calculating the correlations of the social desirability scores with the simple structure scores. By using simple algebraic equations, we can predict in advance what these correlations will be.

Suppose there are only two principal axis factor score vectors. It can be proved that the sum of squares of the correlations of the social desirability scores with the simple structure scores is 1 (see the last section in this chapter). If the correlations are equal, then each correlation will be slightly over .7. To the uninitiated, it might seem discouraging that after all these elaborate computations on the cognitive tests, the simple structure dimensions still correlated more than .7 with the social desirability scores. If there are four factors and the correlations with the social desirability scores are all equal, these correlations will be precisely .5 with each of the simple structure factor scores. Thus one may have a perfectly respectable factor analysis of a set of cognitive items in which the question of social desirability has not been raised and yet have correlations of .5 for each of the cognitive scales with the social desirability factor.

Edwards (1964), who has conducted so much research in the area of social desirability for personality scales, has recognized the relationship between the social desirability factor and the first principal axis of a set of personality dimensions. It is surprising that much of the work in the area of intelligence measurement has not recognized explicitly the relationship between the concept of intelligence as a unitary factor and the first principal axis of a set of intellectual or cognitive variables.

SOCIAL DESIRABILITY AND ITEM MEANS

The connection between the social desirability concept and the first principal axis factor loadings is of fundamental significance. Perhaps increasing emphasis on the relationship of these two phenomena would clarify even further some of the problems in the measurement of personality dimensions. The results already observed are not surprising and make sense from both a mathematical and psychological point of view. Another phenomenon which Edwards (1964) has discussed in connection with item preference values for dichotomously scored personality items is also important. He has found high correlations among the social desirability scale values of the items and their preference values as determined from the responses of individuals to them. This means that for dichotomously scored items, the means and the social desirability scale values of the items tend to be highly correlated. Since social desirability scale values and first principal axis factor loadings also tend to be highly correlated for personality type items, we should expect item means and the first principal axis factor loading elements to be highly correlated.

As a matter of fact, this high correlation between item means and first principal axis factor loading elements has been found in a number of studies. This may be regarded as a curious result because the first principal axis factor loading vector is a function of the correlation matrix which by definition is independent of the means of the variables involved. If one has a set of items with multiple response alternatives such as 1 to 5, then item preference generalizes to item means. For two-choice items, the preference values of the items are precisely their means.

One can also investigate whether item means for multiple response element sets tend to be correlated with the first principal axis. Such investigations were made on one set of experimental data reported in later chapters. It was found that for five-choice items, the item means for items with positive loadings were on the average higher than those for negative loadings. This might indicate that the social desirability variable was contaminating the factor determination of personality dimensions, even though the item means had been mathematically removed from the data before the first principal axis factor loadings were calculated. If, however, we take the grand mean of all the item responses and reverse the scoring of items whose mean is below this grand mean, we get another set of means for the items whose scoring is so reversed. If we now plot all the item means against the absolute values of the first principal axis factor loadings, we would have difficulty rationalizing any positive correlation between the two variables. As it turns out in our experiment, the correlation is essentially zero. However, the instructions given to the subjects on whom the data are based did not call for absolute judgments as instructions ordinarily do. Rather, a relative judgment was called for.

In summary, it is probable that the relationship between item means and the first principal axis factor loadings can be accounted for in terms of direction of scoring for some of the items in the set. One might even take the signs of the first principal axis factor loadings as indications of the social desirability values of the items. It is, however, probable that the factor of social desirability is of less importance than has been suspected and that it may be usefully regarded as a centroid or first principal axis. Appropriate scoring reversals of certain variables and competent rotational procedures may greatly reduce the influence of the social desirability variable in the measurement of personality dimensions.

INTERRELATIONSHIPS OF SOCIAL DESIRABILITY ESTIMATES

We have discussed in some detail the manifestations of a group of statistical phenomena that may be called social desirability indices. One of these indices is a set of values obtained by one of the traditional scaling procedures in which a group of individuals is used to determine scale values of a set of stimulus elements with reference to some designated thing or attribute. Another is the set of item means found when a set of items is administered as a self-report instrument to a group of individuals. A third is the first principal axis factor loading elements of a matrix of item scores.

In many studies consistently high relationships are found among these three sets of values determined for a specific set of stimulus elements. We are led to conclude with Edwards (1964) that in view of such high correlations, these three sets of values must have much in common. We have also in earlier discussions called attention to the relationship between the scaling of attributes and the scaling of entities in a data matrix. If we recall that the ideal scaling procedure integrates the scaling of entities and attributes and that the scaling of attributes is the same thing as the factor loadings for a set of stimulus elements or other variables, then it is not surprising that relatively crude methods for scaling variables or stimulus elements should give results somewhat comparable to those of more sophisticated methods.

We also remember that the first principal axis factor loading for a variable can be reversed in sign simply by reversing the scoring of the variable, and that the preference value of an item is the mean value if the item is dichotomous. A sign reversal gives the complement of the preference value. It is not surprising, then, that for a set of items that has a wide range of preference values on either side of the 50 per cent point, we get a high correlation between the first principal axis factor loadings and the preference values of the items.

FAKING OF ITEM RESPONSES

We have already discussed at some length the problem of getting people to respond to items in a way that is characteristic of their personality rather than in the way they think they should respond. We have identified this phenomenon as the problem of getting the subject to regard himself as a part of the stimulus element rather than to consider the item in relation to an ideal subject. We have also suggested that one of the problems in eliciting responses that are characteristic of the subject is the fact that he may not know himself well enough to give accurate responses. There may be methods by which the subject can be helped to form more accurate and relevant judgments about himself. In this section we shall discuss further some techniques for achieving this end and also for making it more difficult for the subject to give false responses. We shall give further attention to the forced choice technique. We shall also discuss how instructions might assist in these objectives, and how the introduction of certain dummy items in the sets might help in obtaining more relevant responses.

FORCED CHOICE FORMAT

The forced choice format requires the subject to react preferentially to a pair of items each of which has about the same social desirability scale value. Such procedures can be useful if it is assumed that the tendency to give the socially preferred response should be suppressed and not used in the measurement of personality dimensions. The discussion of the previous section suggests that the contaminating effects of the socially desirable variable may be less objectionable than is sometimes feared.

It may be that for some applications of personality inventories certain dimensions are more important than others. For example, in the case of sales jobs, applicants may be preferred who rate high on a dimension which might be called social aggressiveness. The applicant might then tend to mark positively those items intended to assess social aggressiveness. It is possible, however, that if such items were paired with items measuring other dimensions of personality, in situations where the objectives of the examination were not so clear, the tendency to mark the socially aggressive items in preference to other types of items would not be so strong. In general, if a subject is given a personality inventory as a basis for assessing his various personality dimensions, there should be no particular reason why he should prefer to be higher on one dimension than on another. Therefore, the forced choice technique may be useful in suppressing the social desirability factor in situations where the test is not being taken to gain admittance to a particular job activity. It must be emphasized, however, that the forced choice technique yields measures of intra-individual differences for a set of traits rather than measures of inter-individual differences for a given trait. In the one case, a subject is rated on relative strengths of the traits within himself irrespective of other persons, whereas in the latter case he is rated on each of the traits relative to other members of a specified group.

The forced choice format results in ipsative measures and has the effect of removing the first centroid or principal axis from the measures. When this is removed, procedures for rotating to simple structure are not appropriate and the available objective methods do not yield positive manifolds or readily interpretable results.

USE OF NONFUNCTIONAL OR DUMMY ITEMS

A simple device for obscuring the traits to be measured by a set of items is to include a limited number of items selected at random that will not be scored for any of the scales. Such items can serve as "red herrings" for those who are tempted to beat the test. As a matter of fact, in almost any item selection and scoring strategy or technique, a number of items from the original pool will almost certainly have negligible importance for all of the scales. Such items may be retained in the final instrument to make the task of beating the test more difficult.

INSTRUCTIONS TO EXAMINEE

The forced choice format may suppress in part the tendency to react to the socially desirable aspects of personality items, but by its use information which enables one to compare the subject with others of a specified group is lost. It is possible, however, to provide instructions that may assist and encourage subjects to respond to the items as genuinely and sincerely as they are capable of doing. One device is to have the subject compare himself with what he regards as the standard or norm of behavior with reference to a particular item. For example, instructions may be somewhat as follows: "This booklet contains a number of statements about things people do. Read each statement and decide how often it applies to you by selecting one of the following five choices: 1. Much less often than most people; 2. Less often than most people; 3. About as often as most people; 4. More often than most people; 5. Much more often than most people. You are to indicate your choice by filling in the appropriate space on the separate answer sheet. For example, if the statement were 'I read detective stories' and you decide that you read detective stories less often than other people, then opposite the statement number on the answer sheet you would blacken between the lines under the number that corresponds to your choice. Remember that by filling in the appropriate space on the answer sheet you are to indicate for each statement how often it applies to you compared to other people you know." These instructions attempt to encourage the subject to compare himself with other people he knows rather than to make an absolute judgment.

A questionnaire may be administered repeatedly but under different sets of instructions or response sets. For example, the subject can be asked to respond to the items (1) as they apply to him, (2) in the most socially desirable manner, (3) in the way he wishes that they applied to him, and so on. One use to which such studies are put is to see to what extent different results are obtained for different response sets to the same objective stimulus elements. It may be, however, that the general technique of varying response sets can be used as a technique for getting more accurate self-appraisals. In typical experiments with response sets, items are administered first under one response set, then under another. A person might, however, be required to respond to each item according to a number of different response sets before going to the next item. A group of response set elements for each item might be arranged so that a person would be required to indicate his rank order for each item response set. For example, he might be given the response elements as follows: "As it applied to me; as it applies to the ideal person; as it applies to the average person; as I wish it applied to me." If an item applies less to him than to the ideal person, the average person, and so on, he would give the self-reference alternative the lowest ranking, and if it applies most, the alternative would be given the highest rating. In such a structuring, the reference mode of a three-dimensional matrix would be ipsatized. Such ipsatization may not adversely affect normative measurement for the individual, even though it does not yield normative measures for the reference mode.

SCALING THEORY AND PSYCHOMETRICS

We have discussed in previous chapters the importance of integrating scaling and psychometric theory, and have indicated that factor analytic techniques can achieve this objective. We have shown how the early scaling techniques of Thurstone applied to rating situations in industrial organizations. In *The Prediction of Personal Adjustment* (Horst et al., 1941), Guttman further extended the concept of scaling theory to the basic structure of a data matrix of responses to dichotomous items. Guttman did not pursue this concept. He has subsequently used nonmetric methods that are outside the scope of this book.

The synthesis of general scaling theory and psychometrics can be considered as a special case of the approximation of a data matrix to one of lower rank. We shall discuss this concept in terms of categorical sets, problems of metric, problems of scale, and problems of origin.

CATEGORICAL SETS IN DATA MATRICES

A special case of categorical sets occurs with the conventional data matrices in which entities and attributes are the two sets. This two-category data matrix has major relevance for the integration of scaling and psychometric methodology in factor analysis. However, we are not limited to two sets. We may also have occasions, or repetitions of the entity-attribute sets for a number of successive intervals in time. The number of sets may be extended further (Horst, 1965) to include conditions of measurement and types of measuring instruments. The concept of multiple sets was discussed by Cattell (1952) and later elaborated by him in his model of the "data box."

An ingenious rationale and methodology for the analysis of multiple sets of data have been developed by Tucker (1963). His method assumes a core matrix of much smaller dimensions than the multimode data matrix of the empirical observations. The term "mode," used by Tucker in the same sense that we use "category," may have advantages over the latter designation, which could be confused with binary metrics.

One important type of categorical set is that of repeated measurements, a special case of the occasion mode. We indicated earlier that the preferred method of measuring reliability or consistency is by repeated measurements. There may be only two occasions, the first and second administration. The use of this additional mode for the construction of multidimensional personality scales is exemplified in later chapters of this book and its implications discussed in somewhat more detail.

PROBLEMS OF METRIC

Some of the mathematical procedures for transforming quantitative observations in scaling theory indicate the importance of the metric problem. For example, the normal curve has played an important role in psychological measurement theory and practice for many years. Psychophysical and scaling procedures have made assumptions about the true distributions of sensory discriminal ability, intelligence, and other traits. Most scaling and psychometric problems can readily be formulated so that the stimulus elements elicit binary responses.

As a matter of fact, any data matrix can be expanded into a binary data matrix. This expansion is accomplished for each variable by treating each possible value of the variable as a binary variable. Thus, for each of the original variables there will be a set of binary variables equal in number to the number of possible values the original variable can take. For such a set of binary variables, a person is assigned a value of zero for all but one of them. He is assigned a value of one on the binary variable of the set corresponding to his score on the original variable. Very little has been done in the way of investigating properties of such expanded binary matrices which represent completely matrices whose elements are any real numbers. One comes in the limit to the case of continuous measures. At this point the number of members of the attribute sets also becomes infinite.

The problems of metric concern not only the extent to which data are grouped into class intervals of equal size, but also the extent to which nonlinear transformations such as logarithmic, exponential, or trigonometric are introduced. Such transformations imply class intervals of varying size. They have implications for factor analytic procedures and therefore for measurement and scaling procedures in general, but we cannot explore them extensively in this book.

PROBLEMS OF SCALE

We have referred briefly in the previous paragraph to nonlinear transformations of variables. We may also have simple linear transformations, one of which involves a multiplicative constant. Matrices of correlations are not affected by scaling operations on the original variables, for by definition such operations cancel out in the calculation of the correlation coefficients. However, the basic structure of a matrix of correlations or covariances is a function of the scaling applied to such matrices. The basic structure of a correlation matrix is no simple function of the basic structure of the covariance matrix and the standard deviations from which it was derived. That these relationships are not simple is important for both scaling and measurement techniques. In factor analysis it has been customary to use correlation coefficients rather than covariances. However, factor analytic techniques are available that are independent of scaling constants (Horst, 1965).

PROBLEMS OF ORIGIN

One of the simplest transformations of variables is a change in the origin of measurement. For example, requiring that the smallest number assigned to a response element should be zero implies a change of origin. Tucker (1958) has presented an example from learning data in which origin is important. He points out that one may be interested in following the progress of persons over successive trials. If in a matrix of entities and trials we deviate the measures by entities, information of major interest is low. For such matrices Tucker has recommended that the raw score matrix be used as the basis for factor analysis. There may be other cases where the problem of origin is of crucial importance and where one may not, without loss of important information, use deviation rather than absolute measures. The basic structure of data matrices varies with changes of origin by entities, by attributes, or both. In *Factor Analysis of Data Matrices* (Horst, 1965), we give limiting values of the basic diagonal elements or eigenvalues as functions of the origin vectors and the original basic diagonals.

MATHEMATICAL PROOFS

FIRST PRINCIPAL AXIS FACTOR LOADINGS AND SIGN CHANGES

Let X be a raw score matrix consisting of two sets of variables such that

$$X = (X_1, X_2) \tag{6.1}$$

Assume that for the second set we get another matrix of scores by subtracting each score from a constant, thus

$$Y = c1\ 1' - X_2 \tag{6.2}$$

where c is a constant. We let

r_{11} be the correlation matrix for the X_1 variables,
r_{12} be the correlation matrix for the X_1 with the X_2 variables,
r_{22} be the correlation matrix for the X_2 variables,
r_{1y} be the correlation matrix for the X_1 with the Y variables, and
r_{yy} be the correlation matrix for the Y variables.

We let

$$R = \begin{bmatrix} r_{11} & r_{12} \\ r_{21} & r_{22} \end{bmatrix} \tag{6.3}$$

$$\rho = \begin{bmatrix} r_{11} & r_{1y} \\ r_{y1} & r_{yy} \end{bmatrix} \tag{6.4}$$

$$i = \begin{bmatrix} I & 0 \\ 0 & -I \end{bmatrix} \tag{6.5}$$

where corresponding submatrix orders are the same in all three matrices. It is readily proved then that

$$\rho = iRi \tag{6.6}$$

Let the basic structure of R be

$$R = Q\Delta^2 Q' \tag{6.7}$$

From Equations 6.6 and 6.7

$$\rho = iQ\Delta^2 Q'i \tag{6.8}$$

Let

$$iQ = Q_\rho \tag{6.9}$$

From Equations 6.8 and 6.9,

$$\rho = Q_\rho \Delta^2 Q_\rho' \tag{6.10}$$

But Equation 6.10 is in basic structure form since iQ is orthonormal. The principal axis factor loading matrix of R is by definition

$$a = Q\Delta \tag{6.11}$$

and of ρ

$$a_\rho = Q_\rho \, \Delta \tag{6.12}$$

From Equations 6.9 through 6.12

$$a_\rho = ia \tag{6.13}$$

Equation 6.13 shows that changing the direction of scoring of the X_2 variables gives the same principal axis factor loadings as for the original score except for change of sign.

CORRELATION OF FIRST PRINCIPAL AXIS FACTOR SCORES
WITH SIMPLE STRUCTURE FACTOR SCORES

Let y be the matrix of normal principal axis factor scores and u the matrix of simple structure factor scores such that

$$u = yH \tag{6.14}$$

where H is square orthonormal. Then the matrix of correlations of the principal axis factor scores with the simple structure factor scores is simply

$$r_{y'u} = y'u \tag{6.15}$$

By definition

$$y'y = I \tag{6.16}$$

From Equations 6.14, 6.15, and 6.16

$$r_{y'u} = H \tag{6.17}$$

The vector of correlations of the first principal axis factor scores is

$$r_{y._1'u} = H_1.' \tag{6.18}$$

and the sum of squares of these correlations is, from Equation 6.18,

$$r_{y._1'u} \, r_{y._1u} = 1 \tag{6.19}$$

In particular, suppose the social desirability scale values of the variables are defined as the first principal axis factor loadings, and the social desirability scores of the persons as the first principal axis factor scores. Then Equation 6.19 shows that the sum of the squares of the correlations of the social desirability scores with the simple structure factor scores must be 1.

CHAPTER **7**

Technological Problems

7n Chapter 6 we considered a number of problems in the construction of a personality instrument that must be considered before it is administered to an experimental group. In this chapter we shall consider problems concerned with processing the data matrix so that we may determine objectively the dimensions of the system and solve for the scores of persons on these dimensions. These problems include computer limitations, the number of factors, and transformation procedures.

COMPUTER LIMITATIONS AND SOLUTIONS

We have already indicated that adequate multiscale test construction technologies must use computer facilities. The role of the computer will be discussed and illustrated more fully in Chapter 9. In this section we shall consider some typical technological issues involving the use of computers, including external data storage, external program storage, packing and unpacking techniques, matrix transposition, obverse analysis routines, and models involving matrix partitioning and supermatrix construction.

EXTERNAL DATA STORAGE

In Chapter 1 we discussed the use of external storage units to supplement core storage or immediate access memory. Many programs written for computers assume that both the data and the program can be held in core storage, but the data matrices yielded by experiments designed to determine and measure the dimensionality of personality variables are typically too large to be contained in core storage. Therefore, external data storage such as tapes and disks must be provided. The efficient use of these units requires considerable skill, ingenuity, and technical knowledge. One must know the number and designations of tapes and the capacity of disk files. The input and output tape units, as well as the unit used for punching computer data on cards, are not available to the user for intermediate storage or "scratch." Other tape units may be reserved for the operation of the system. The peripheral storage capacity of many computer installations may well be taxed by the requirements of a large data matrix program using factor analytic procedures such as is described in later chapters.

EXTERNAL PROGRAM STORAGE

In previous paragraphs we discussed the use of peripheral storage units for storing data in various stages of the computation procedures. However, it is sometimes necessary to use tapes also for storing parts of the program. This may be the case when the program is so long that there is not enough space left in core for the necessary computations, even though the maximum use of peripheral storage is made for data storage.

A type of external program storage is available for FORTRAN IV. This procedure is called *overlay*. In the overlay procedure, an additional program called the *main program* calls the links of a program, stored on tape, as these links are required in core. The links are referred to in the statements as subroutines. However, they differ from conventional subroutines in that they do not require a list of the variables used in the subroutine. Furthermore, in the standard subroutine procedure the subroutine is stored in core along with the calling program. In the overlay system, special control cards are required for each of the links or subroutines called by the main program. The main or calling program remains in core at all times. It is therefore desirable that the calling program be as short as possible and restricted as nearly as possible to the calling of subroutines. However, it is often necessary to include simple computational or control statements in the main program.

It is important to maintain optimal balance between the use of core space and the time required for transmitting between core and tape the various links or subroutines in the program. In overlay programs the core space reserved for dimensioned variables in the main program should be kept at a minimum.

PACKING AND UNPACKING

One serious limitation of all standard large computers is the fact that they have, in effect, fixed word length. Where this word length is not long enough, it is possible by double precision arithmetic to combine two storage locations and thus double the number of digits in a word. This capability is useful in the physical sciences which require ever greater accuracy. For the social sciences, on the other hand, the need is for much greater core capacity for words with few digits.

Normally, each separate storage location has assigned to it only one number, whether that number has nine digits or is binary. For many data matrices in psychology, the elements are either 0 or 1. In the analysis of binary data there is a tremendous waste of core space when a single-bit word or number is assigned to a location of thirty-six or more bits.

The ideal computer would have one-bit word lengths and any specifiable order of multiple precision. It may be that the technological and circuitry problems involved in such a hardware structure are insurmountable. On the other hand, it is probable that the tremendous usefulness of such flexibility has not been sufficiently recognized.

There is, it is true, a way of utilizing more fully the capacity of a single storage location. By appropriate mathematics and programming, it is possible to get up to thirty-two one-bit words into a thirty-three-bit word length storage location. This is called *packing*. The packing procedures enable one to get optimal use from the available bits in core storage. In these procedures, one determines the maximum integer value that will appear in a set of data, and how many numbers of this magnitude can be put into a single location. Ordinarily, packing procedures are simplest if integers are used, but one can go readily from integers to decimal numbers and vice versa. Of course, all numbers that are packed into a single word, if they are to be manipulated individually, must also be unpacked at times during the computations. Programs are available (Horst, 1966b) for the packing procedures used in the storage and application of integer response weights for scoring a data matrix for each of a number of dimensions of personality variables developed.

Like the data and program storage procedures involving external units, the packing and unpacking techniques also involve trade-off considerations with reference to storage and time. The amount of space that can be saved by packing binary words may be of the order of magnitude of 30. Where with conventional methods one can reserve up to 18,000 or 20,000 words in core for the storage of a data matrix, one might in the same space store 600,000 elements of a binary data matrix, since each element would require only one bit.

The advantages of the packing procedures are offset by the additional time taken to unpack the elements of the stored matrix as they are required for computation. Ordinarily, the packing requires only one set of operations, and even though this can be somewhat lengthy, once it is done it need not be repeated. However, if iteration procedures are used as, for example, in calculating the simple structure factor loading matrix from the raw data matrix, then many cycles of unpacking are required for the computations. Therefore, although the concept and the procedures for packing and unpacking as a way of saving space in storage are most attractive, the practical applications for such procedures are limited.

MATRIX TRANSPOSITION

One of the simplest operations in matrix manipulation is that of matrix transposition. This operation is so primitive that mathematicians have neglected to emphasize it as an important operation among the set of operations that can be performed upon matrices. One of the most important applications of matrix transposition is in the manipulation by computers of very large matrices such as concern us in this book.

The concept of transposition assumes relatively little importance when all of the computations can be handled in core. But if the matrix is very large, as in the case of typical data matrices, and if operations are to be performed repeatedly upon both the matrix and its transpose, then it is necessary to have both the matrix and its transpose on peripheral units. With most data matrices, the data are read into the computer by entity vectors. If the number of variables is very large, then one typically may store the matrix by row vectors on tape as they are read into core. Each record on tape is therefore a row. The problem is to get the matrix on tape so that each record is a column. This then would be the transpose of the matrix. Methods for putting both a very large matrix and its transpose on tape are now available (Horst, 1966b).

OBVERSE FACTOR ANALYSES

It has been traditional in factor analysis methodology to begin with a correlation matrix. The factor analysis performed on the correlation matrix yields some sort of factor matrix, presumably a principal axis matrix. This is then typically transformed into a simple structure matrix. From the simple structure matrix we can calculate a factor score matrix for the particular sample from which the factor loading matrix was calculated. Such a set of solutions implies solutions for the basic orthonormals and the basic diagonal of a data matrix, or what have been called (Horst, 1963, 1965) its basic factors.

The conventional methods imply that one is interested only in the basic diagonal and the right orthonormal of a standardized data matrix. However, from a purely formal point of view, in the methods of solution for the basic structure factors of a data matrix the orientation of the matrix is entirely arbitrary. It is well known (Horst, 1963, 1965) that one can solve first for either of the orthonormals and the corresponding basic diagonal. Then the other orthonormal can be solved for as a function of these two matric factors and the data matrix.

It is curious that psychologists have made so much of what has been called the obverse factor method. To psychologists it makes a great deal of difference whether one places the emphasis on people or on tests. This distinction may be interesting psychologically, but it is not relevant for computational purposes. Whether or not the obverse method is used depends mainly on considerations of computational economy.

The time required for solving for the basic structure or latent roots and vectors of a Grammian or product moment matrix increases at least as the square of the order of the matrix. The calculation of the remaining orthonormal, irrespective of which of the two is solved for, takes much less time. Obviously then, that procedure which yields the smaller product moment matrix is the preferred one. Therefore, if the number of cases is much smaller than the number of variables, one would use the obverse method.

These assertions assume that in both the direct and obverse methods, the metric of the data matrix will be the same. For example, if one uses a matrix of standard measures for the direct method, then one would also use the same matrix of standard measures for the obverse method. These discussions also assume that the communality issue is circumvented by excluding specific factors from the model of the factor analysis. Thus far, no adequate treatment of the obverse solution has been presented when specific factors are postulated. As a matter of fact, the concept of specific factors and communalities has not been sufficiently well defined mathematically to enable one to formulate it adequately and generally for both the direct and obverse solutions.

PARTITIONING AND SUPERMATRICES

Another operation on matrices that has not been sufficiently emphasized by mathematicians is matrix partitioning and super-matrix construction (see Horst, 1963). In matrix partitioning we segregate submatrices within a matrix by indicating separations between certain rows and columns of the matrix. The simplest case is the type III supervector (Horst, 1963) where a matrix is partitioned either by rows or columns to yield a column vector or a row vector whose elements are themselves matrices. This operation has important applications for matrix manipulation by computers when the matrices are very large (see Chapter 9).

We may also consider a number of matrices all having the same number of rows or the same number of columns. Such matrices may be arranged in row or column order to yield a type III supervector whose elements are matrices. All submatrices in a row have the same number of rows and all submatrices in a column have the same number of columns. It is important to distinguish between the partitioning of matrices and the construction of super-matrices, a distinction generally ignored by mathematicians.

Methodology and computational procedures have been developed (Horst, 1966b) which use the concepts of matrix partitioning and supermatrix construction for the computer manipulation of matrices too large to be stored in core and for which computations on the complete covariance matrix are far too time-consuming for practical purposes. This procedure is discussed in Chapter 9.

DETERMINATION OF THE NUMBER OF FACTORS

We indicated earlier that one objective of factor analysis is to determine the minimum number of things we should investigate in a particular area or domain in order to cover it adequately. A number of different criteria may be used for deciding when we have enough factors. These we shall discuss in terms of the test reliabilities, the smallest eigenvalue, the percentage of variance accounted for, arbitrary or rational determinations, hypotheses as to the number of factors, significance tests, and finally, an excess number of factors.

TEST RELIABILITIES

Suppose we have a number of different measures on a group of persons, such as reactions to a large number of personality items or test scores on a large number of different tests. If the tests were administered a second time to the same group, presumably the results would not be precisely the same. This is what we have referred to as retest reliability. The reliability estimates that may be calculated from the two sets of measures may be used as an index of the systematic variance of the variables in a particular sample. The sum of the reliabilities of the individual variables may be taken as an estimate of the total *true* variance of the set of measures. The remaining variance is assumed to be *random* or unsystematic. We assume that it is this chance or random variation that accounts for less than perfect correlations between two administrations of a test. In general, the principal axis method indicates, for any particular data matrix, how much of the total observed variance is accounted for with a specified number of factors. The reliability coefficient is the variance of a set of true measures whose observed variance is unity. Reliability coefficients may therefore be used as an aid in determining when enough factors have been extracted to account for some specified proportion of the reliable variance in the set.

This use of reliability coefficients assumes, of course, that we have two sets of measures on the same variables for the same group, and raises the question of how these two sets of measures shall be used in the factor analysis. Several possibilities are available. We could, for example, conduct a separate analysis on each set and get two different sets of results. We could also consider each replicated variable as two variables, one for each administration, and conduct a factor analysis which would give us factor loadings on a number of factors for each variable for the first and second administrations.

On the other hand, we could treat each of the replications as two different individuals. Then we could solve for factor loadings for each of the tests, and for factor scores for each of the individuals for both the first and second administration. The latter method is used in this book because it yields a single factor loading matrix and ultimately a single weighting matrix for obtaining factor scores. This procedure yields a single unambiguous scoring matrix for calculating factor scores from a multiscale personality inventory.

Retest reliability coefficients may be used in several ways to determine how many factors to solve for. In this book we simply compare the total sum of reliabilities with the total amount of variance accounted for to indicate how much of the systematic variance has been accounted for. It is possible to set up more elaborate procedures in which the total amount of variance that each variable accounts for in the set of factors calculated is approximately proportional to the reliabilities of these variables. Such methods of factor analysis have not been well developed nor have computational procedures been provided.

SMALLEST EIGENVALUE

A criterion that has been proposed for determining whether enough factors have been calculated is that the variance accounted for by the last principal axis factor vector calculated shall not be less than one. This variance is, of course, the eigenvalue corresponding to the factor vector. This criterion is applied to factor analyses of correlation matrices where by definition the variance of each of the variables is unity. The rationale here is that no principal axis factor should be retained which accounts for less variance than that accounted for by any of the variables. Since the factors are presumed to give a parsimonious representation of a much larger set of variables, presumably each retained factor should account for more variance than any one of the variables.

This criterion of unity assumes that unities have been used in the diagonal of the correlation matrix. The use of communality estimates in the diagonal precludes the use of the unit eigenvalue criterion. Unity probably represents a lower limit to the variance which a retained factor should account for, and will in general yield more factor vectors in the principal axis matrix than should be retained in the final simple structure solution.

PERCENTAGE OF VARIANCE ACCOUNTED FOR

In most factor analytic studies, one finds that the first principal axis accounts for a high percentage of the total variance of the set. For example, if there are ten variables, the first principal axis may account for 40 per cent of the total variance, and the first three factors may account for 80 per cent or more of this total variance. A practical procedure is to set an upper limit for the percentage of the total variance to be accounted for by the factors, such as 75 per cent. The percentage may be determined in part by a knowledge of the reliabilities of the variables. One may decide, for example, that the total variance accounted for need not be greater than 80 per cent of the reliable variance of the system. In this case, if the average reliability coefficient were, say, .6, then one would not attempt to account for more than 48 per cent of the total variance of the set. The criterion of percentage of variance accounted for is largely subjective. There are no clear guide lines or criteria for establishing such percentages. These are arbitrary, just as is the value of unity for the smallest eigenvalue or factor variance.

ARBITRARY OR RATIONAL MAXIMUM NUMBER

In the programming of factor analysis procedures for computers, it is sometimes desirable to indicate an upper limit for the total number of factors one will allow for any particular set of data. Such upper limits may be of more practical than theoretical significance. If limits are not set, then one may, for a particular job, find that the computer keeps grinding away at the unit eigenvalue criterion or some percentage of variance criterion, and devours much more computer time or money than is available for that job.

There are, however, certain general limits for the number of factors, based on both theoretical and experimental evidence, which are useful. For example, in the pioneering studies of Thur-

stone on intelligence factors, the number of interpretable and practically significant factors did not exceed more than ten or twelve.
In studies of personality items and tests, the number of factors has
not been more than twelve to fifteen. Even in the study described
in this book where twenty-four factors were postulated, it was not
possible to get more than about twelve interpretable factors. To
date, no serious attempt has been made to assemble a large number
of different types of measures to include all the dimensions of personality and intelligence that one might think of as a basis for determining the total dimensionality of measurable human behavior.
But for the separate analyses that have been conducted in the personality and cognitive domains, it is probably significant that the
number of recognizable and reasonably clear-cut factors which
emerge is rarely more than twelve.

The methods by which these factors have been obtained vary
greatly, and the criteria for when to stop factoring have been by no
means uniform. Even though some investigators have claimed to
get up to fifty factors, these factors have not been calculated from
a single matrix. They come from subsets of factor analyses which
are later synthesized by a priori procedures. It is probable, therefore, even in spite of the prolific ingenuity of psychologists to generate labels for concepts, that because of the vast redundancies oc-
curring among these labels, the total number of factors from any
given study that can be even roughly interpreted will not be more
than fifteen or twenty. Perhaps, therefore, one might use thirty as
the maximum number of factors to be calculated in a single study.
The procedures developed in this book provide for a maximum of
fifty factors.

HYPOTHESES AS TO TOTAL NUMBER OF FACTORS

The foregoing discussion implies that one may have a hypothesis as to the total number of psychological factors to be found
in any battery of variables that might be assembled, even if each
variable is restricted to a single item yielding a dichotomous measure. For many years the author has hypothesized that one could

account for perhaps 80 per cent of the nonrandom variance of measures on any number of socially significant variables with not over thirty factors. With this number it is still difficult to guess what all of these factors might be. An estimate of fifty factors as an upper limit is probably rather generous. However, a FORTRAN IV computer program is now available which will handle up to fifty factors (Horst, 1966b).

Many psychologists shrink from the notion that there should be an upper limit to the number of primary dimensions of behavior which may be profitably investigated. This antipathy to a parsimonious structuring of the discipline of psychology is difficult to understand. Certainly in the physical and biological sciences, one of the major objectives is the achievement of parsimony. However, this criterion arouses rebellion among many psychologists who prefer to be given full semantic rein without the rigorous constraints imposed by scientific methodology.

SIGNIFICANCE TESTS

One cannot discuss the number of factors to be solved for without introducing the subject of significance tests. Mathematical statisticians have devoted a great deal of attention to testing the significance of the eigenvalues or roots of a correlation or covariance matrix. The distribution functions of such roots have been investigated at some length. Presumably these distributions are functions of the number of cases in the study; if one had a total universe there would be no sampling distribution for these roots. But significance tests based on the traditional models of mathematical statistics do not appear to be relevant for deciding when to stop factoring. Even if one had available the total universe, whatever that could possibly mean, and the latent roots for a given correlation matrix based on this group, one would not use nearly all the factors even though by definition they would all be significant. Mathematical statisticians have not taken adequately into account in their models the distinction between errors of measurement for the members of a sample and sampling errors due to selection of samples from populations. Until more adequate models are built by the statisticians, it is doubtful whether the significance tests provided by them will be useful in determining the number of factors to be solved for.

EXCESS NUMBER OF FACTORS

We have discussed a number of different criteria for deciding how many factors to solve for. Some of these criteria are vague and subjective. At the risk of being more vague, one may say it is probably better to solve for too many factors than for too few. In the simple structure transformed factor loading matrix, it may be difficult to interpret the factors if not enough principal axis factors have been solved for. If one has solved for too many principal axis factors, then in the simple structure matrix calculated by the varimax transformation procedures or other similar methods, some of the factors will not be clear-cut or interpretable. These then may be discarded. No systematic studies have been conducted to determine how many principal axis factors should be used in the transformation so that maximum clarity of interpretation will result in the simple structure factors. Such studies might prove empirically useful in establishing more objective criteria. In any case, there seems to be little question that it is better to solve for more principal axis factors than one needs for his final results rather than too few.

TRANSFORMATION AND KINDS OF FACTORS

We mentioned in Chapter 3 the implications of transformation procedures on the arbitrary or principal axis factor loading matrix as a basis for labeling the factors and for getting factors that will make for more effective communication among specialists and between specialists and laymen. We shall consider in further detail some of the technological issues involved in the determination of transformations for the principal axis matrix to the simple structure matrix. These we shall discuss in terms of orthonormal transformations, oblique transformations, communication effectiveness, the transformation matrix itself, the implication of transformations for suppressor items, and the normalization of factor loadings.

ORTHONORMAL TRANSFORMATIONS

We referred in Chapter 5 to orthonormal transformations for the principal axis factor matrix. Such transformations guarantee that the simple structure factor scores are mutually orthogonal in the sample. There is sometimes confusion as to what is meant by orthogonal factors. Whether we have "orthogonal factors" depends on how we define this term. Perhaps the only meaningful interpretation is that the factors are orthogonal if the factor scores derived from the factor loading matrix are uncorrelated. One of the best known procedures for calculating an orthonormal transformation matrix is the Kaiser varimax transformation (1958) which maximizes the variance of the squares of the factor loadings. In this book we present a modification of Kaiser's computational procedure that is particularly adapted to the transformation of very large factor matrices.

OBLIQUE TRANSFORMATIONS

Thurstone (1947) preferred transformations which are more general than orthonormal transformations, and analytical procedures have been developed for calculating such oblique transformations (Harmon, 1967). The obliquity of a transformation may yield second order general factors and subsequently first order general factor loadings and first order general factor scores. If one adopts this model, which seems to be the only respectable model for the general factor hypothesis, then he cannot assume the obliquity to be characteristic of the sample and the simple structure matrix to be characteristic of the tests. The oblique solution introduces complications not encountered with orthogonal transformations in the use of factor scores as predictor variables for external criteria.

COMMUNICATION CONSIDERATIONS

The objectives of invariance with reference to samples of entities and attributes seem to be more fundamentally important than that of communication as such. Only to the extent to which communication is important in all scientific endeavors are the labeling advantages resulting from transformation procedures important. This point of view is admittedly not consonant with the widespread interest of psychologists in using factor analysis in semantic enterprises for generating labels.

TRANSFORMATION MATRIX

In many factor analysis studies, it is traditional to present the transformation matrix itself as an important and interesting component of the factor analytic computational results. If the transformation is indeed oblique, then the transformation matrix itself is of interest in that the correlations of the primary factors may be calculated from the transformation matrix. These correlations are of interest primarily as they imply general factors in the model. It is in the further analysis yielded by the oblique transformation matrix that second order factor loadings, and then first order factor loadings and factor scores, may be calculated. The procedures for calculating these are presented in *Factor Analysis of Data Matrices* (Horst, 1965). If the transformation is by fiat orthonormal, then this transformation matrix is not of particular interest as such. It is a function primarily of the particular variables included in the study.

SUPPRESSOR ITEMS

The general inverse of the simple structure matrix calculated by means of the orthonormal transformation will typically include a large number of negative weights. This will be the case even though all variables are scored in a positive direction and the first principal axis factor loadings are all positive. The traditional psychometric concept which emphasizes the importance of having homogeneous items within subscales of a multiscale instrument and heterogeneous items among subscales is not particularly relevant for the general factor analytic approach. One advantage of this approach is that one need not be greatly concerned about constructing subsets of items that correlate high among themselves and low from one set to another. The main consideration is that the total set of dimensions be well represented by the items. The general factor analytic approach then enables one, by the use of suppressor items, to compensate for the inability to achieve the ideal of within-subset homogeneity and between-subset heterogeneity. It has become increasingly evident that this ideal of classical measurement theory is very difficult if not impossible to achieve in practice. Whether it is worth trying to achieve is debatable.

NORMALIZATION BEFORE TRANSFORMATION

We have already considered some of the more detailed considerations involved in normalization by rows of the factor matrix. Computational procedures are simplified if the principal axis factor matrix is not normalized before application of the varimax transformation. If it is desired to have normalized test vectors in the factor matrix, then it is probably better to build such constraints into the factoring method (see Horst, 1965) rather than to impose them on less sophisticated approximation procedures.

CHAPTER 8

Methodological Problems

*I*n Chapters 6 and 7 we discussed problems that have been grouped for convenience into psychological and technological issues. In this chapter we shall consider another type of problem characterized primarily by the particular model or underlying set of constructs that provide the basis for the rationales and computational procedures of the following chapters. These problems include the concept of categorical sets or modes, configural analysis of data matrices, the simplex phenomenon in personality measurement, and the communality problem.

CATEGORICAL SETS

In our previous discussions of categorical sets we suggested a number of different kinds of modes or sets that may be relevant in psychology, and indicated some implications of the multidimensional set for the measurement of personality dimensions. In this section we shall restrict our discussion to the three-mode set consisting of entities, attributes, and occasions. These are particularly relevant for the determination of personality dimensions. Suppose we have measures of a set of attributes on a set of entities or persons for each of two or more administrations of the instrument. Then we may construct a three-dimensional matrix in which one dimension is entities, another attributes, and the third occasions. We may consider three different ways of reducing the three-dimensional set to a two-dimensional set. We shall discuss the entity-occasion versus the attribute set, the attribute-occasion versus the entity set, the entity-attribute versus the occasion set, alternative two-dimensional reductions, the problem of scaling, and finally the three-mode set.

ENTITY-OCCASION VERSUS ATTRIBUTE SET

We may consider slabs from the three-dimensional matrix such that each slab is an occasion and the dimensions of the occasion slab are entities and attributes. One may construct a supermatrix of these slabs, placing one above the other in a plane to give a type III column supervector (see Horst, 1963) which in simple form has as many columns as there are attributes, and the number of rows is the product of the number of occasions by the number of entities. This is now a two-dimensional data matrix. We can perform a factor analysis which gives a factor score matrix for the entity-occasion dimension and a factor loading matrix for the attribute dimension. Such an analysis assumes that each person is a different person from one occasion to the next. To the principal axis factor loading matrix of attributes, one may apply a transformation procedure and get a simple structure factor matrix. One may then get the general inverse of this factor matrix and use it as a weighting matrix to get factor scores for each entity on each occasion for each simple structure dimension. Suppose the analysis had been applied to the standardized data matrix. Then the product moment matrix of the type III supervector of factor scores would by definition yield the identity matrix.

We may also calculate the supermatrix of factor score correlations among the subsets of occasions. We should not expect the submatrices of correlations for the occasion sets or for the various pairs of sets to be identity matrices. However, the extent to which these approximate identity matrices would indicate the degree of orthogonality we might expect in subsequent applications of the weighting matrix to other samples. The diagonal elements of the off-diagonal submatrices would give an indication of the retest reliabilities of the factor measures. The procedures implied in this discussion are used in this book.

ATTRIBUTE-OCCASION VERSUS ENTITY SET

Considering once more the cube of data matrix elements, we may again take slabs so that each slab is a different occasion. But now we can arrange the slabs side by side in a type III row supervector which in simple form will have the same number of rows as entities and the same number of columns as the product of occasions by attributes. We may consider the basic structure of such a matrix in which the left orthonormal represents the principal axis factor score matrix for persons. The right orthonormal represents a type III row supervector in which the submatrix elements are the factor loading matrices for each administration of the attributes. In this case, we regard each administration of the test as a different test.

Suppose now we wish to get a weighting matrix from the factor loading matrix which can be applied to the data matrix for getting factor scores. The procedure is not clearly indicated by the supermatrix of factor loading submatrices. If later we wish to evaluate the factor scores for a person from a single set of test responses, there is no obvious way of using the supermatrix of factor loading matrices as a basis for such a scoring procedure. Therefore, we conclude that this method for ordering the data matrix does not yield a suitable multidimensional factor scale weighting matrix.

ENTITY-ATTRIBUTE VERSUS OCCASION SET

Going back again to the cube of data matrix values, we may consider slabs such that each slab is an attribute and its dimensions are entities and occasions. In this case, we could arrange the slabs one above the other so that in simple form the supermatrix would have an occasion for each column, and the number of rows would be the product of the number of entities by attributes. Here again, the basic structure solution is implied. If we assume that successive occasions should give the same results except for error, then one may regard the matrix just considered as a rank one matrix and assume that subsequent factors are error factors.

ALTERNATIVE TWO-DIMENSIONAL REDUCTIONS

One may also arrange the attribute slabs in row type III supervectors, so that the simple form of the matrix would have as many rows as there are entities and as many columns as the product of the number of occasions by the number of attributes. This matrix is the same as the one considered under "The Attribute-Occasion versus the Entity Set," except that the ordering is first by attributes and then by occasions within attributes. Obviously, this ordering consists of a permutation transformation that does not affect the values obtained in the basic structure solution; only the order in which they occur is affected.

If slabs are taken from the data matrix cube so that each slab is an entity, these slabs may be ordered in one of two ways. In the first, the simple form of the matrix has as many rows as there are occasions and as many columns as the product of the number of entities by attributes. In the other, we have as many rows as attributes and as many columns as the product of the number of occasions by entities. It can readily be seen, however, that by transposition and permutation operations, these two matrices can be reduced to those previously considered.

PROBLEM OF SCALING

In all arrangements of the slabs of the cube of data matrix elements, some assumption about the scaling of the original data must be made. Presumably, since the attributes are not necessarily measured in terms of comparable units or origins, the original scaling should take place with reference to the attributes. Two choices are possible. One of these is to take standard measures for the combined entity-occasion set for each attribute. The other is to take standard measures for the columns of entities separately for each occasion and each attribute. The procedure used in this book is the former.

THREE-MODE DATA MATRIX

Arrangements of the three-mode data matrix which yield two-dimensional matrices give three different kinds of solutions. Each of these yields a basic orthonormal whose distinct order is the same as one of the modes. The distinct order of the other orthonormal is the product of the orders of the two remaining modes. In Tucker's (1963) three-mode type of analysis, three different two-mode matrices are connected by a three-dimensional core matrix whose dimensions correspond to the number of entity, attribute, and occasion factors. The two-mode matrices and the core matrix are determined so that a specified function of their elements yields an acceptable approximation to the three-mode data matrix.

Such an approach to the analysis of data from a multi-mode experimental design suggests the integration of psychometric and scaling theory with developmental, learning, and experimental psychology. The entity and attribute modes correspond to psychometric and scaling theory. The occasion mode corresponds to learning and developmental theory, and the condition mode to what is loosely called "experimental psychology."

This more general approach, however, goes beyond our immediate interest in the development of multidimensional personality scales. For this purpose, the relevance of the three-mode data matrix is that the special case of two occasions yields retest reliability estimates of the items which can be useful in determining the number of systematic nonchance factors in the system and provides estimates of the retest reliabilities of the factor scales.

CONFIGURAL ANALYSIS

The concept of configural analysis has evolved because of the conviction among investigators that a summation or even a weighted sum of individual responses to a set of stimulus elements does not necessarily give all of the relevant information obtainable from these responses about the responding individual. In this section we shall discuss the implications of configural analysis for the measurement of personality. We shall consider the nonlinear hypothesis, the mathematics of configural analysis, and the factor analysis of configural variables.

NONLINEAR HYPOTHESIS OF CLINICAL PSYCHOLOGISTS

For many years clinical psychologists, as well as others, have contended that the number of correct answers to a set of personality items, where "correct" has been more or less arbitrarily determined, does not necessarily yield a meaningful score. It has been emphasized that one can get the same score from a number of different response patterns. The greater the number of items, the more different ways it is possible to get the same score. Certainly it is reasonable to assume that marking correctly a particular ten out of twenty items in a test might have quite a different meaning for a person than marking correctly the other ten in the test. Clinical psychologists and psychiatrists have contended that the dynamic interrelationships of the various possible responses to items may be significant for a particular client. Responding positively to a pair of items might have special significance distinct from that of responding positively to one or the other of the items. Meehl (1950) called attention to this possibility some years ago. However, the generalization of the concept to various combinations of items was not considered in detail by him. The author has pointed out (1964b) that what came to be known as Meehl's paradox could be expressed mathematically as a simple nonlinear equation in the binary item variables.

MATHEMATICS OF CONFIGURAL ANALYSIS

Meehl's paradox is a special case of a more general mathematical function. This function is the general multivariate polynomial. It expresses relationships among patterns or configurations of responses in a much more precise manner than had been done in the empirical studies of pattern analysis by McQuitty (1956) and others.

One may express a total score as a sum of item scores, as in Equation 8.1:

$$S = X_1 + X_2 + \cdots + X_n \tag{8.1}$$

Here it is seen that we simply have a sum of the scores for each of the variables. If the item scores are binary, then the total score is simply the number of items correctly answered. A slightly more complicated way of calculating the scores is indicated in Equation 8.2:

$$S = a_1 X_1 + a_2 X_2 + \cdots + a_n X_n \tag{8.2}$$

Here the total score is not merely a sum of the scores on the individual variables but rather a weighted sum of these values. A coefficient or weighting value is associated with each score for the variable.

Both Equations 8.1 and 8.2 are linear combinations of the item scores. It is the mere counting operations implied by Equation 8.1 when the scores are dichotomous that many persons object to when they say that the whole is not equal to the sum of the parts. This is the sort of objection which Gestalt psychologists have raised against atomistic psychology.

However, one need not be restricted to these simple linear relationships. Suppose we have a set of scores for a person. From such a set we can generate additional numbers—which are not merely sums or weighted sums of these numbers—by taking products of all distinct pairs of these numbers. We can also take the products of all distinct triplets of such numbers. And so, for each person, we can take the product of all distinct combinations of such numbers up to the product of all of the numbers. In this way, we can generate for each person a large number of additional values that are not linear combinations but rather product combinations of variables in the original set. These procedures have been discussed by the author (1964b), by Osburn and Lubin (1957), and by Wainwright (1965). Equation 8.3 gives the general form of the multivariate polynomial which is a linear function of the first order variables and all possible higher order products of these variables:

$$S = a_0 + a_1 X_1 + \cdots + a_n X_n + a_{12} X_1 X_2 + a_{1n} X_1 X_n$$
$$+ \cdots + a_{(n-1)n} X_{n-1} X_n + \cdots + a_{1..n} X_1 \cdots X_n \quad (8.3)$$

Therefore, we have the possibility of generating many new values that are not linear functions of the old and that give indices of the interactions of the variables in successively higher order combinations.

FACTOR ANALYSIS OF CONFIGURAL VARIABLES

We have then a straightforward analytical procedure for including in a set of measured variables higher order interactions that enable us to represent mathematically all of the information which can be taken into account by less sophisticated empirical methods of pattern and configural analysis. Having generated a set of variables that contains all of the interaction or configural information available in the original set and that is much larger in number than the original set, we may now consider a factor analysis of this set of data. Whether these more elaborate analyses would yield useful and interpretable information about personality dimensions and useful personality scores has not been thoroughly investigated. The work of Wainwright (1965) indicates that systematic variation can be introduced into sets of personality items by generating higher order interaction variables.

One of the difficulties with higher order interaction variables is the fact that the sheer number of possible configural variables for even a small number of items can be overwhelming. However, recent analytical procedures and computer developments, together with the specific procedures developed in this book, suggest that much more definitive analyses will be possible for configural variables. Procedures are now available (Horst, 1966b) which make it possible to analyze a data matrix of up to 6,000,000 elements. The application of factor analytic techniques to configural variables may therefore open up new vistas for research in the definition and measurement of personality dimensions.

THE SIMPLEX IN PERSONALITY MEASUREMENT

A special case of what Guttman (1958) has called the simplex in correlation matrices can result from binary data matrices. In this section we shall consider the special case, then the general case and its factor analytic implications, multidimensional measurement aspects, nonlinear factor analysis, and corrective suggestions.

SPECIAL CASE OF THE SIMPLEX

We are familiar with the simplex which can occur when the items are scored dichotomously. The mathematical properties of data matrices exhibiting the simplex phenomenon have been discussed by Guttman (1958) and by the author (Horst, 1964a). One objection to conventional methods of factor analysis of test items is the fact that, even though the items are perfectly homogeneous, the correlation matrix cannot be of rank one if the item means are distinct. If two items have different proportions, the Pearson product moment correlation or phi coefficient cannot be unity. It is obvious, by looking at an ordered binary data matrix exhibiting the perfect simplex, that one could not find two vectors whose major product moment yields such a matrix. This has caused Guttman (1958) to object to conventional factor analyses of such matrices. He has shown that one can express the elements of a correlation matrix resulting from a simplex type data matrix as functions of parameters equal in number to the number of distinct proportion values for the items. He has emphasized that one cannot, however, reproduce such a matrix of correlations as the major product of a single factor vector. The mathematics of the case is obvious. The conclusion that factor analytic techniques are not appropriate for single-item variables with binary scores is not so obvious or compelling. One may argue that even though the mathematics is incontrovertible, the best rank one approximation may be justified. Factors subsequent to the first may be regarded as artifacts of the binary metric. However, it is probable that this simple solution will eventually be replaced by a more adequate and sophisticated model.

GENERAL CASE

It is readily proved that a correlation matrix for a perfect simplex type of binary data matrix must have rank equal to the number of distinct values. The implications of this fact have not been so evident in the case of variables whose measures are the sum of dichotomous values. The more general case of the phenomenon of multiple rank based on considerations of frequency has been implied by Carroll (1961). It has been recognized for some time that it is possible to get a perfect positive correlation between two variables only when the frequency distributions for the two variables are the same. Having given the frequency distributions for two variables, Carroll has shown how the maximum possible correlation between them can be calculated. The argument, therefore, that one should not do conventional factor analyses on matrices from dichotomous variables because of the phenomenon of disparate proportions applies more generally to any set of variables for which the distributions are not identical. This criterion would exclude virtually all cases of measured variables. We must therefore either reject the application of factor analysis, and perhaps even correlation analysis, to data matrices in general, or live with the phenomenon of factors generated by disparate distributions or peculiarities of metric.

MULTIDIMENSIONAL MEASUREMENT AND SIMPLEX

One may conceive of a model consisting of subsets of items where each subset exhibits a perfect simplex. The scores for the subsets are simply the number of items correct. Assume that by appropriate sequential arrangement of entities the simplexes exhibit identical distributions. If this sequential ordering of the persons in all of the scales were to put them in the same order for all scales, then obviously the distributions of test scores would all be identical and the correlations among the scores would be perfect.

Let us see now whether the same simplicial subsets with identical distributions could also yield a matrix of zero correlations among the subscale scores. This amounts to asking in how many ways a set of numbers can be rearranged so that the rearranged sets will correlate zero with one another. A system of rearranged sets yielding a matrix of zero correlations appears to be the paradigm for sets of perfectly homogeneous subscales with maximum heterogeneity among the scales. The simplest case occurs with only a single item. Having given a binary vector with a specified number of 1's in it, in how many ways can the elements be rearranged to give new vectors so that the scalar products of all of the vectors are equal? The answer to such a question could be answered empirically, and perhaps analytical methods could be developed for the more general cases where the possible outcomes are not limited to binary values.

In any case, while the concept of the simplex for binary measures has been extensively studied for a single set of measures, it has not been investigated for the case of multiple simplexes within a set of data. The problem has been formulated by Bloxom (1966), and several lines of development are suggested by him.

NONLINEAR FACTOR ANALYSIS

Perhaps one of the most interesting and ingenious developments in factor analysis in recent times is the model of nonlinear factor analysis developed by McDonald (1967). This model begins with a single factor score vector, and assumes that subsequent factor score vectors are polynomial functions of the first. For example, it assumes that the second factor score vector is a second-order polynomial function of the first, the third is a third-order polynomial function of the first, and so on.

The successive factor vectors may be more complicated functions. The first order of complication assumes that there are two independent factor loading vectors in the set. The third factor loading vector may then be a second order multivariate polynomial function of the first two. Successive factor loading vectors may be higher order multivariate polynomial functions of the first two. We may then proceed in this fashion to attempt to account for all of the factor score vectors found in a principal axis solution. The first

159

two factor score vectors are not necessarily principal axis solutions, but may be some other function of the principal axis solution. One may also assume three or more independent factor score vectors and then attempt to express other vectors as multivariate polynomial functions of these.

CORRECTIVE SUGGESTIONS

We have seen how with binary variables the simplex phenomenon may introduce multiple factors into a Guttman-type scale. The nonlinear factor analysis approach may prove useful in resolving the dilemma posed by Guttman (1958) and give a welcome alternative to his proposal for abandoning conventional methods of factor analysis. In his discussions of the simplex, Guttman does not offer a solution to the problem of the reproduction of the data matrix with a number of parameters equal to the sum of its dimensions. Presumably any system for factoring a correlation or product moment matrix should also enable us to express the data matrix from which it was derived in terms of a comparable number of parameters. A number of methods have been suggested (Horst, 1965) for partialing out the simplex from a set of data so as to leave a reasonably pure representation of the true dimensionality of the system. No entirely satisfactory solution has yet been demonstrated. In the procedures in this book, we assume that the peculiarities of metric which capriciously or systematically influence the number and kinds of factors obtained are not sufficiently great to invalidate the results. In general, it is probably safe to assume that the factors with smallest variance may be regarded as due in part to measurement error and in part to variance generated by the disparate distributions of the variables.

Any satisfactory method of factor analysis should provide adequately and rationally not only for the factor loadings of the tests but also for the factor scores of the individuals. While the latter cannot be done with the methods of Guttman (1958), it might be done with the nonlinear factor methods developed by McDonald (1967).

THE COMMUNALITY PROBLEM

We shall consider the communality problem in terms of optimal data matrix approximation, epistemological considerations, and the concept of parsimony.

OPTIMAL DATA MATRIX APPROXIMATION

If we wish to reproduce as accurately as possible with a given number of factors the normalized measures of a sample of subjects on a set of variables, this can be achieved by applying the principal axis method to the correlation matrix with unity in the diagonals. More precisely, suppose we have a normalized data matrix from which we calculate a correlation matrix. From the correlation matrix we calculate a principal axis factor loading matrix for a number of factors less than the number of variables. We then divide each principal axis factor loading vector by the root mean square of its elements to get a new matrix. Next we multiply the standardized data matrix by the new matrix we have just calculated. This gives a factor score matrix whose height is the same as the normalized data matrix and whose width is the same as the number of factors. If now we postmultiply this factor score matrix by the transpose of the principal axis factor loading matrix, we get another matrix whose order is the same as that of the normalized data matrix but whose rank is equal only to the number of factors. Next we subtract this new matrix from the normalized data matrix to get a difference matrix. Finally, we get a scalar quantity which is the sum of squares of the elements in the matrix of difference elements.

We can now state categorically that within limits of decimal accuracy this scalar quantity is less than or equal to the sum of squared elements of a difference matrix obtained by subtracting from the normalized data matrix any other matrix whose rank is equal to the number of factors. To achieve this minimum sum, one must use unity in the diagonals of the correlation matrix. If one has objectives other than the most parsimonious description of the data matrix, objectives that require the use of communalities in the diagonal, then this should be explicitly stated and the procedures justified. It is not enough to say that one wishes to use communalities so that the correlations can be reproduced with fewer factors.

EPISTEMOLOGICAL CONSIDERATIONS

By definition the specificity of a variable, such as a test or item, plus its communality is the total nonerror variance of the variable. If a test has zero or very low correlations with all of the other tests in the battery, then this test has by definition a low communality and high specificity. Suppose the test is reasonably reliable and that we construct six other reliable tests very much like the first. These tests can be made as much like the first test as we please by including in them items which are in the first test. Suppose the items in the tests are sufficiently overlapping so that the correlations among the six are, let us say, .7. In a factor analysis of the augmented battery, the specificity of the first test would be much lower than it was before the similar tests were introduced. This merely means that the specificity of a test depends on the particular battery in which it is placed.

Specificity then is not a characteristic of a test but rather of the battery in which the test is placed. In a personality test, we should include a number of different items to measure the same primary personality dimension. This in general is not difficult to do; if one assembled a very large number of personality items it would probably be difficult to find any one for which redundancies could not be found elsewhere in the set. One could readily collect a set of items such that no one of them would be specific with reference to the particular set.

Therefore, when behavior items are used to measure personality dimensions, there appears to be little justification for postulating specific factors that imply the use of communality estimates in the diagonal of the correlation matrix. Actually, if the principal axis solution and varimax transformation are applied to a matrix of correlations with unity in the diagonals, a variable with high specificity will yield a varimax factor loading vector in which only that variable will have a significant loading. One could eliminate such variables and factors from further consideration.

However, the elimination of variables after the factor analysis is completed may require a reanalysis of the remaining variables. Such procedures are much more costly and time-consuming than those which do not eliminate variables. Nonfunctional items might better be left in a test to help obscure the scales within it and thus reduce the tendency for persons to make socially desirable responses.

SPECIFICITY AND PARSIMONY

We have already pointed out that to postulate both specific and common factors violates the principle of parsimony. Such a model yields more factors than the number of variables from which they were derived. Some philosophical approaches emphasize the uniqueness of events. Science is much less concerned with identifying differences among events than in finding the minimum number of parameters, principles, or laws to account for the maximum number of different phenomena.

CHAPTER 9

Computer Utilization and Test Construction Technology

We shall now attempt to summarize in perspective the basic assumptions of the personality test construction technology implied by the preceding chapters, and examine the crucial role of the computer in the implementation of the technology. Our basic assumptions are based on the following propositions:

1. The instrument consists of a large number of stimulus elements.

2. The stimulus elements represent a wide range of socially significant behaviors.

3. Responses to each of the stimulus elements are readily and objectively quantifiable.

4. The instrument is administered to a large group of persons.

5. A large data matrix is generated by the administration of the instrument in which each column represents a variable or item, each row an entity or person, and each element the score of a person on an item.

6. The data matrix can be adequately approximated by the major product of a factor score matrix and a factor loading matrix whose common order is small compared to the number of items and persons.

7. A factor loading matrix can be found which will satisfy adequately the criteria of simple structure.

8. The set of items that have high loadings in a given factor are such that a group of competent judges can reach an adequate consensus on a label for the set.

9. The scoring matrix by means of which factor scores are obtained is defined as the general inverse of the factor loading matrix.

10. The product of the data matrix and the scoring matrix is the matrix of factor scores.

11. The scoring matrix with appropriate scaling, origin, and truncation adjustments is used to get factor scale scores for persons not in the experimental group. This matrix is the essence of the test construction technology implied by this book.

It is urged that any multiscale test construction technology is adequate only to the extent that it satisfies at least implicitly the foregoing assumptions.

The underlying mathematical rationale for the reduced rank data matrix approximation is well known (Horst, 1965). This rationale is fundamental to satisfying adequately the foregoing assumptions. The major practical considerations in implementing the technology are primarily computational. To the extent that any multiscale test development enterprise fails to use the maximum available computer capabilities, to that extent does it fail to be an optimal procedure. To better appreciate the validity of this assertion, let us return to assumptions 1, 2 and 3. These have to do with the size of the data matrix from which the scoring matrix is developed.

Let us assume that we hypothesize a domain of fifty factors. This is from three to four times more factors than have been identified with reasonable confidence in any competent study of personality traits to date. Nevertheless, we may assume that to be as inclusive as possible we have assembled and constructed items to cover up to fifty labeled behavior characteristics. Irrespective of how much overlapping or redundancy we may have, to be satisfied that each of these characteristics has been adequately represented, assume that we have twenty items for each hypothesized trait or factor. This gives a total of 1000 variables. This is less than twice the number of items in the Minnesota Multiphasic Personality Inventory. Some studies in recent years have included up to 3000 items.

Let us assume further that in order to have a very stable determination of the factor variables and the scoring matrix we obtain a sample of 1000 persons. Assume also that in our analysis we wish to incorporate information on the short-term temporal stability of the items. We therefore administer the 1000-item form twice to the sample of 1000 persons. If we regard each of the two occasions for each person as a separate entity, this means that finally we end up with a 2000 by 1000 data matrix. From this matrix we then wish to develop a scoring matrix for the 1000 items on a number of scales which presumably will not exceed fifty and probably will not be greater than fifteen or twenty. Somewhere in the procedure we imply the factor analysis of a 1000 by 1000 correlation or covariance matrix. The number of items and persons may well exceed 1000 so that the matrix would be even larger. In any case, the end result will be a scoring matrix with the number of rows equal to the number of items and the number of columns equal to the number of factors. It is quite possible that some of the rows of this matrix will turn out to have all zero or negligible size elements. Such rows will indicate items that can be eliminated from the multifactor scale since they carry little if any weight for any of the factors.

In any case, a basic structure type solution of gigantic proportions, or at least some adequate approximation to such a solution, is called for. Even if the number of variables and cases is much smaller, say, 500 persons and 300 items, the computational requirements for the development of an adequate scoring matrix are still very great. No satisfactory solution is feasible without the use of large-scale computer facilities. To gain some appreciation of the nature and extent of the computational requirements, we shall consider some of the more obvious approaches that can be used and relate these to the computer facility requirements. The methods we shall discuss are: large data matrix iterations from tape, correlation matrices on tape, the multiple group method from a large correlation matrix, the successive elimination of data vectors, clustering from a simple structure matrix, and matrix partitioning and supermatrix construction. Tape is interpreted here to mean any peripheral storage unit.

LARGE DATA MATRIX ITERATIONS FROM TAPE

The successive principal axis vectors can be calculated directly from the data matrix (Horst, 1965). We shall discuss this method in terms of the procedures, the tape requirements, and the time requirements.

PROCEDURES

Calculation of the principal axis factor loading matrix directly from the data matrix, without going through the intervening operations of calculating the correlation matrix, uses the iteration procedures developed by Hotelling (1933) and modified by the author. The correlation matrix can be expressed as the minor product moment of a normalized data matrix. We define a normalized data matrix as one in which the means of the columns are zero and the standard deviations are the reciprocal square root of the number of cases.

The procedure begins with the calculation of the normalized data matrix. This matrix is then stored on one tape by rows and on another by columns. It is possible to store the matrix by rows on the first part of a tape and then the transpose on the same tape. However, a single tape may not hold both a very large matrix and its transpose.

The Hotelling iteration procedure begins by multiplying the correlation matrix by an arbitrary vector. The resulting vector is then scaled by some convenient constant and the resulting scaled vector is used as a multiplier for the correlation matrix. This procedure continues until the vector stabilizes or until some specified tolerance limit is reached. Once the vector has stabilized and been scaled to the principal axis factor loading vector, the major product moment of this vector is subtracted from the correlation matrix and the iterations are repeated on the residual matrix. These cycles continue until enough principal axis vectors have been extracted.

In the case of direct operations on the normalized data matrix, one must go through two steps for each iteration of a vector. In the first step, the data matrix is postmultiplied by an approximation to a factor loading vector. The resulting vector is normalized. In the second step, the transpose of the normalized data matrix is postmultiplied by the normalized vector to yield the next approximation to the factor loading vector. These two steps then accomplish what is achieved in one step in the direct application of the Hotelling iteration method to the correlation matrix. It can readily be shown that the normalized vector approaches the principal axis normal factor score vector corresponding to the principal axis factor loading vector (Horst, 1965).

In the two-step procedure requiring the calculation of two vectors, one iterates to both a factor score vector and a factor loading vector. When the iterations are adequate for a given factor, the major product moment of the factor score vector by the factor loading vector is subtracted from both the natural order and the transposed data matrix. The iterations now proceed on this residual matrix. These cycles continue until enough factors have been extracted.

After the principal axis factor loading matrix has been calculated, computations for the varimax simple structure transformation are required. The varimax transformation procedures are independent of those for getting the principal axis factor loading matrix and will not be considered here (Horst, 1966b). In general, they are the same whether one calculates the principal axis factor loading matrix directly from the normalized data matrix or from the correlation matrix.

TAPE REQUIREMENTS

Two tape units are required for a large matrix, one for the data matrix and the other for its transpose. A major consideration in the analysis of large data matrices is the size of the largest matrix that can be stored on a single tape. A larger matrix can of course be stored on a high-density tape which holds between two and three times as many words as a low-density tape. However, the capacity of a single tape does not determine entirely the maximum size of the matrix that can be used in the program. Disk storage, where available, may provide a larger amount of storage than is provided by a single tape. In this case, one must know the total amount of storage available to the user on the disk file. Where the use of tapes is preferred in computer installations that use disk simulation of tape, one can write routines which specify that the actual physical tapes be used instead of the disk.

It is also possible to use several tapes for the storage of a single matrix and several more for storage of its transpose if the matrix is too large to be held on a single tape. However, a computer program that provides for multiple tape storage of a data matrix is more complicated than one that uses only one. Another objection to the allocation of several tapes to a data matrix is that the total number of tapes required for the entire program may exceed the number available in even a large computer installation.

There is a more serious disadvantage to the use of actual tape units rather than disk simulation. The computational procedures implied by the method require so many iterations of multiplication of the data matrix and its transpose by a vector that a tape may be worn out from reading and rewinding long before the iterations are complete. For example, if an average of twenty iterations is required for each of twenty factors, this means that a tape must be read and rewound 400 times before the solution for the principal axis matrix is complete. Tapes cannot be expected to survive even a fraction of this abuse.

Two symbolic tape designations are typically required for storing the data matrix and its transpose, and the successive residual matrices. A third tape is required for calculating the residual matrices. In programs for handling very large data matrices, the use of core storage should be reserved almost entirely for computations, since little space will be available for data storage as such. A tape will therefore be required for storage of the principal axis factor loading matrix as the successive vectors are calculated. The varimax solution also requires an additional tape for storing the varimax factor loading matrix. Thus a minimum of five tape designations is required for handling the calculations in the direct procedure based on the normalized data matrix.

TIME REQUIREMENTS

It should be obvious from the discussion of tape usage that time requirements may be great. Since the data matrix and its transpose are both on tape, each of these must be read into core every time the two-step iteration is performed for the original matrix and the successive residual matrices. By far the greatest amount of time required for the set of computations that eventually yields the scoring matrix is for the calculation of the principal axis matrix. The time required for the varimax transformation matrix is of a much lower order of magnitude than for the principal axis factor matrix. Therefore, our consideration of time requirements will be devoted mainly to the calculation of the principal axis matrix.

Let us assume that we have a data matrix with 1000 cases and 1000 variables. Obviously, to multiply such a matrix by a vector implies 1,000,000 multiplications. Remembering that we must also multiply the transpose by a vector to get a given approximation to a principal axis vector, this means that for each approximation we have 2,000,000 multiplications. We also have the same number of additions, since each product must be added to a previously cumulated sum. Four million computations are therefore required for the calculation of each approximation to a principal axis factor vector. Suppose we allow an order of magnitude of 60,000 computations per second, and remember that some additional computations are required for the scaling operations. The time required for a given approximation to a factor loading matrix is then of the general order of magnitude of seventy seconds per approximation. This is perhaps a reasonable estimate on the IBM 7094. If we have twenty iterations for each factor and twenty-five factors, the order of magnitude of the time to calculate the principal axis vectors is ten hours.

Unfortunately, however, this figure accounts for only the computational time. The time required to read a word from tape or to write it on tape is roughly ten times as long as that for making an addition or multiplication, and the number of words that must be read is about half the number that must be multiplied or added for a single iteration. This means that the reading time is roughly five times as long as the computational time. With buffer storage we assume that no time is lost in the computations. Thus the total time is roughly five times the computational time or about fifty hours for the calculation of twenty-five factor loading vectors from a matrix of 1000 by 1000. If one increases this by a factor of 20 to 50 per cent for the additional calculations required for matrix normalization, the varimax matrix, the scoring matrix, and the factor scores and their intercorrelations, the order of magnitude may well be seventy hours for a 1000 by 1000 matrix. For higher speed and greater capacity computers, the time could of course be substantially less.

CORRELATION MATRICES ON TAPE

Obviously much of the time taken in calculating the principal axis factor loading matrix directly from the normalized data matrix is due to the two steps required for each iteration. For a square data matrix, for example, the amount of time required for an iteration is about twice that required with the correlation matrix. But additional time is required for the calculation of the correlation matrix.

For 32K storage, the maximum number of variables that can be handled in core without the use of auxiliary tapes is between 200 to 225. Even for this number it is necessary to use space efficiently by dimensioning only a single array for the matrix and calculating only the nonredundant elements of the correlation matrix. This makes for somewhat more complicated programming. The procedures for doing this are given in *Factor Analysis of Data Matrices* (Horst, 1965).

PROCEDURES

As for the direct solution from the data matrix, we may first calculate the normalized data matrix. This, however, is not necessary. We can calculate the minor product moment of the raw data matrix and store it on tape. We can then bring it back into core, a vector at a time, and by means of well-known formulas calculate the corresponding vector of correlation coefficients. This procedure assumes that enroute we have calculated the vectors of means and standard deviations, which is easy to do if the raw data matrix has been stored on tape.

As indicated in *Matrix Algebra for Social Scientists* (Horst, 1963), we can express the product of two matrices as the major or minor product moment of type II supervectors. This means that we may express the product as a sum of major products of vectors or as a matrix of scalar products of vectors. The distinction between these two methods of computing matrix products is not traditionally recognized by mathematicians but is important for planning strategies of computer calculations. The former approach has advantages for small matrices that can be held in core. But if one uses the sum of major product moments of row vectors as the computational scheme, then for very large correlation matrices it is necessary to partition the row vectors of the data matrix so that successive submatrices of the product moment matrix can be calculated. Such a procedure is probably unjustifiably complicated from the point of view of program writing, and no more rapid than the alternative procedure of calculating the product moment as a matrix of minor products of column vectors of the data matrix. We shall therefore assume this latter procedure.

If we calculate the minor product moment of either the raw data matrix or the normalized data matrix as the major product moment of a type II supervector, then it is necessary to have both the natural order and the transposed data matrix on tape. A subroutine for the transposition of large matrices has been written (Horst, 1966b). It is also necessary to store a duplicate of the transposed matrix on another tape so that the two can be independently manipulated.

To begin the product moment computations, the first vector from the first tape is read into core. Then the first record from the second tape is read into core and the minor product of the two is calculated. The next record from the second tape is brought in and written over the first record from that tape. The product moment of the two vectors in core is calculated. Holding the first vector of the first tape constant, one proceeds through all of the vectors of the second tape, calculating the product moment of these with the first record of the first tape. One then has a vector of the elements of the first row of the product moment of the data matrix. This is read out on a third tape. The second tape is then rewound. The second record of the first tape is then read into core over the first record and one proceeds through all the records of the second tape as before and writes the second row of the product moment matrix on the third tape. One proceeds in this way until all vectors of the product matrix have been calculated and written on the third tape.

This procedure implies a reading and rewinding of the second tape as many times as there are columns in the data matrix. It is possible to program the computations so that for the constant multiplier matrix more than one vector is brought into core at a time, this number depending upon the size of the matrix. A computer program that has been written for this method (Horst, 1966b) multiplies together very large matrices, each of which is on a separate external storage unit. The number of times the variable tape unit is read and rewound is determined by the size of a submatrix of the constant tape unit that can be held in core. This number is simply the number of these submatrices into which the data matrix may be partitioned.

Depending on the size of the data matrix and the optimality of the multiplication program, there is still a lower limit to the number of operations required to calculate the correlation matrix. For a data matrix of size 1000 by 1000, the minor product moment of this matrix obviously requires for each element 1000 multiplications and 1000 additions. Since there are 1,000,000 elements, this is a total of 2,000,000,000 multiplications and additions. Of course, almost half of these are redundant. One might save some time by calculating only the distinct values, but in doing so one would encounter programming and tape handling complications, since subsequent operations on the correlation matrix require the complete matrix rather than only the triangular part of it. In any case, 2,000,-000,000 multiplications and additions at 60,000 per second might require about ten hours of computational time.

Assuming that we do have the correlation matrix, we may now proceed with the calculation of the principal axis factors according to any approved method. One would almost certainly not use either the Jacoby type methods or the co-diagonal methods (Horst, 1965). Iteration techniques based on Hotelling (1933) would most likely be used, since probably no more than the first thirty basic structure factor vectors would be calculated. Having calculated the principal axis factor loading matrix, one would then calculate the simple structure varimax matrix, the scoring matrix, and perhaps the factor scores and their intercorrelations for the experimental sample.

TAPE REQUIREMENTS

It is not particularly crucial for tape requirements whether the normalized data matrix is first calculated and then the product moment data matrix, or whether the raw score product moment matrix is calculated first and then the correlation matrix. A third tape unit designation is required for storing either the product moment or correlation matrix. If the factor scores and their correlations are not desired, one can use the first two tapes for calculating the simple structure and scoring matrices. As a maximum, five tape unit designations should be adequate for this approach.

It should also be clear that problems of tape durability depend on whether actual or disk simulated tape units are used. The number of readings required for the variable tape unit in the calculation of the product moment matrix could be prohibitively high.

TIME REQUIREMENTS

We have seen that for a 1000 by 1000 matrix it is conceivable that as much as ten hours of computer calculation time alone might be required for calculating the correlation matrix from the data matrix. Even assuming that almost half this time were saved if only the triangular part of the correlation matrix were calculated, and assuming that this shortcut in calculation does not greatly complicate an increase in the time required for additional tape handling operations, the order of magnitude of the time required for calculating the elements of a 1000 by 1000 correlation matrix may still be more than five hours. We are then just ready to begin to calculate the principal axis factor loading matrix. The time required for these operations is shorter than for the direct method discussed in the previous section, because one does not go through the two-step multiplication procedure involving the matrix and its transpose, but at best one could not hope to reduce the computations by more than one half of those required for calculating the principal axis factor matrix directly from the data matrix. There we saw that the time required may be up to seventy hours. The total time required for calculating a principal axis factor loading matrix of twenty-five factors for a 1000 by 1000 data matrix via the correlation matrix could very well be of the order of magnitude of forty hours. If one adds to this additional time for the varimax transformations and other computations, the time could well exceed fifty hours for an IBM 7094 or a comparable computer.

MULTIPLE GROUP METHOD FROM A
LARGE CORRELATION MATRIX

One method of factor analysis that was particularly popular before the advent of computers is the multiple group method. This method was developed by Thurstone (1947) as a shortcut procedure for simplifying factor analysis computations. It is one of the most rapid methods available. Although it is less accurate than the principal axis solution, it yields a rank reduction solution (Horst, 1965). We shall discuss the procedure, the factor scores, tape requirements, and time requirements.

PROCEDURE

The multiple group method can in principle be applied either to the data matrix or to the correlation matrix. In this method we have a binary hypothesis matrix with number of rows equal to the number of variables and number of columns equal to the number of factors assumed present in the data. For each variable and each factor, a 1 appears in the hypothesis matrix if it is assumed that the variable has an appreciable loading in the factor. Otherwise, a 0 appears. It is probably desirable to assume only a single factor for each variable. However, as Thurstone (1947) has pointed out, this is not a necessary requirement of the multiple group method.

The chief problem with the hypothesis matrix is to determine a priori which values should be 0 and which 1. In applying the multiple group method to a very large data matrix, we must remember that the correlation matrix must be on tape. An examination of this matrix might assist in the construction of a binary hypothesis matrix. This would require computer operations since one would scarcely examine visually a 1000 by 1000 correlation matrix. As a clue to the construction of such a matrix, we note that the elements of a binary vector, other things being equal, will have a larger variance than will a vector of values distributed between 0 and 1. We may take as a first approximation to a binary hypothesis one of the vectors from the correlation matrix. We shall choose the one with the largest variance for its elements.

The variance of each of the vectors of the correlation matrix can be calculated by the computer even if the correlation matrix is on tape. We thus get a vector of variances of the vectors of the correlation matrix. We now take the vector that has the largest variance as the first approximation to a binary hypothesis vector. This vector can be located on tape and read into core. We may then decide arbitrarily that the locations of those correlations in the vector which are above one sigma beyond the mean of the correlations shall be assigned values of 1 and the others values of 0. This then will constitute the first binary hypothesis vector.

Next we may exclude from consideration all vectors of the correlation matrix corresponding to those which have 1's in the first binary hypothesis vector. Then we find which of the remaining correlation vectors has the largest variance. This vector can be read into core and a second binary vector established in the same way as the first, with the exception that we exclude in the units position any variables that have unit elements in the first binary vector. In this way we can proceed to determine a binary hypothesis matrix such that no row of the matrix has more than a single 1 in it. Thus each of the variables is allocated to a hypothetical factor.

It is economical of storage space and time to construct a single vector to represent the binary hypothesis matrix as one goes along. This vector has 1's in the position corresponding to the 1's of the first binary vector, 2's in the positions corresponding to the 1's in the second binary vector, and so on. Therefore, a number in this vector indicates the number of the hypothetical factor that the corresponding variable is presumed to measure.

One may now use the binary hypothesis matrix as the arbitrary matrix in the rank reduction solution and solve for the multiple group factor matrix (Horst, 1965). If the major product moment of this factor matrix is subtracted from the correlation matrix, the rank of the residual matrix is less than that of the correlation matrix by an amount exactly equal to the number of factors.

A varimax transformation may now be applied to this matrix and a scoring matrix obtained from the resulting matrix. However, the procedures for calculating both the varimax matrix and the scoring matrix are more complicated than for those based on the principal axis factor loading matrix.

FACTOR SCORES

Two alternatives for obtaining factor scores are implied in the preceding discussion. In one the binary data matrix may be used for clustering or specifying subsets of items that are presumed to measure each of the factors in the system. The other implies the calculation of a scoring matrix from a varimax type factor matrix.

The first of these alternatives is appealingly simple, but several difficulties are encountered. First, we have no guarantee that the distribution of the number of items assigned to each scale will be satisfactory. Some scales may have many more items assigned to them than others. Some scales may have a very few or only one item assigned to them. This problem in assigning items to scales was recognized in Chapter 5. One must then decide whether to throw out factors with too few items. If they are eliminated, what does one do with the items? If a factor is thrown out, then one may decide that the items still should be retained for some other factor. But how to assign them requires additional rationales or procedures. If one simply eliminates factors and items for which the factors do not have enough items, then one may well eliminate many items that may serve useful functions in the multidimensional scale. Furthermore, factor scores calculated on the basis of unit scoring of items assigned to the scales by the hypothesis matrix exhibit intercorrelations that may be undesirably high. In any case, this method, appealing and simple as it may be, does not appear to provide good results in actual practice.

In the second alternative we calculate the arbitrary multiple group factor matrix, the varimax simple structure matrix, and the scoring matrix. Obviously, these matrices will not be the same as the corresponding matrices from the principal axis method. The results will be biased by the particular binary matrix adopted in the solution. This bias occurs with any binary matrix used in the multiple group method. A serious disadvantage of this method is that not all of the correlations have equal opportunity to determine the arbitrary factor loading matrix and the final varimax matrix. Little is known about the nature and extent of these biases.

TAPE REQUIREMENTS

The tape requirements for the multiple group method are of course the same through the calculation of the correlation matrix as for the method described under "Correlation Matrices on Tape." There a minimum of three tapes is required for the calculation of the correlation matrix. If one is interested only in calculating the vector that consolidates the binary hypothesis matrix from the correlation matrix as a basis for segregating the items into scale clusters, then no additional tapes will be required. One of the tapes used for calculating the correlation matrix will handle all necessary peripheral storage. This is true even though one wishes to preserve the data matrix on one of the tapes as a basis for calculating factor scores for the experimental sample later on.

Even if one wishes to calculate the multiple group factor matrix and the simple structure and scoring matrices, the tape requirements are not increased by more than one. Once the correlation matrix has been multiplied by the binary data matrix, the tape for the former matrix is no longer required for preserving the correlation matrix. This tape may then be used for the calculation of the multiple group factor matrix. The maximum number of tapes needed for the multiple group method does not exceed four.

TIME REQUIREMENTS

The time required for the calculation of the correlation matrix is of course the same for either the multiple group method or the method which calculates the principal axis factor loading matrix from the correlation matrix. This we have seen may be up to ten hours on the IBM 7094 for a correlation matrix of order 1000. However, the additional time requirement, whether one stops with the binary data matrix or proceeds from there to the calculation of the multiple group, the varimax, and the scoring matrices, is negligible compared to that required for the correlation matrix. The hypothesis matrix for segregating the items into scales can also be used to calculate scale scores from the data matrix with little additional time. Even the calculation of the multiple group, simple structure, and weighting matrices will not require more than several additional hours.

It is seen that for the methods discussed, the order of magnitude of the time requirement is between twenty and seventy hours for a matrix of order 1000. Such jobs are far larger than those to which standard computer center operations are geared. These time requirements are, of course, based on computers such as the IBM 7094 and the CDC 3600. Even assuming that more advanced computers enable one to increase speed by an order of magnitude of five or ten for a 1000 by 1000 matrix, the methods we have discussed might require two to seven hours. As the size of the matrix is increased, the time increases at least as the square of the order of the correlation matrix. For example, with a 2000 by 2000 matrix, the order of magnitude of time would increase somewhere between 4 to 8. It is probable that even with more advanced computers the time required for the factor analysis of such matrices would be from ten to fifty hours.

SUCCESSIVE ELIMINATION OF DATA VECTORS

Another approach to large data matrix analysis (Tryon, 1965) begins by partitioning the data matrix into submatrices, either by rows or by columns. We shall discuss this method in terms of the procedures and its limitations.

PROCEDURES

We may take subsets of the variables in a large matrix and for each of the subsets perform a factor analysis. On the basis of this analysis, we may assume that a limited number of variables in the subset can be used to represent adequately all of the variables in it. In this way, we find subsets within larger subsets that we can group together in a much smaller total set and again find representative subsets of variables within subsets of the total group. We may arrive at a final subset of variables which is believed adequately to represent or characterize the total set of variables with which we started.

The procedure can also be applied to subsets of cases or entities so that one progressively reduces the entities to a much smaller group which is thought to be adequately representative of the total group of entities in the original matrix.

Presumably in this way one can reduce either the length or the breadth of the matrix to a set of variables and entities which is manageable within available core storage capacity and requires a limited amount of peripheral storage. One may then solve for the factor loadings of eliminated variables as functions of the factor loadings of the selected variables and their correlations with those eliminated (Horst, 1965).

We have said that by some means the total set of variables is divided into subsets. One may assume the subsets are sufficiently small to be analyzed within core. One could, for example, conduct a varimax factor analysis for each of the subsets and retain for each factor only that variable which had the highest loading in it. Thus one would retain only as many of the variables in the subset as there are varimax factors. One would of course restrict the total number of factors solved for within a subset to assure that this number was much smaller than the number of variables in the subset.

Other criteria for selecting the variables could be used. For example, those with the smallest communalities could be eliminated. One may begin by specifying that the subsets should be restricted to not more than seventy, eighty, or ninety variables for each subset. One can further specify that the total number of factors solved for in a given subset should not be more than twenty. After the first round, one may have only a fourth as many variables as he started with. After the second round, he might also have a fourth as many as he began with on that round. In this way, the total number of variables in a set can be reduced at a rapid rate from one round to the next. At the end of the third round, one might have only one sixty-fourth as many variables as he had to begin with. If the original number were 1000, then at the end of the third round only twenty-five variables would remain. This would ordinarily be too small a number of variables to use in a factor analysis, but we might reasonably assume that those which survive do indeed adequately represent the total set with which we started.

Having given this twenty-five-variable set, one might find that it had only twenty significant principal axis factors in it. One might now find the correlations of these variables with the remaining variables that had been eliminated. This would not require an unrealistic amount of work. Having given the principal axis factor loading matrix of the twenty-five variables, one could then estimate this factor loading matrix for the remaining variables in the set of 1000 or more variables. One might use one of the several available methods (Horst, 1965) for calculating the factor loading matrices from incomplete correlation matrices. In any case, one could then arrive at some arbitrary factor loading matrix that could later be transformed to a varimax matrix and this in turn to a scoring matrix.

LIMITATIONS OF METHOD

This general approach obviously has built-in capabilities for rapidly reducing the number of variables or entities and for then estimating the factor loadings of all the variables. The chief disadvantage of the method is that it places increasingly more and more dependence on less and less information from the total set of variables. It is true that some of this information is used in the construction of the final factor loading matrix, but not until after much information has been lost from the excluded variables. The method exaggerates the disadvantage of the procedure outlined in the multiple group approach where similarly most reliance is placed on the variables selected at each stage by the binary hypothesis vector. All the information given by the intercorrelations of the excluded variables with one another is ignored.

CLUSTERING FROM SIMPLE STRUCTURE MATRIX

We saw in Chapter 5 that the simple structure factor matrix may be used as a basis for clustering items into factor scales. This method assumes that each cluster or subset of items measures a different factor or dimension of personality. We shall review briefly the procedure and indicate some of the results.

PROCEDURE

The most obvious procedure for identifying variables to be included in a cluster from the simple structure matrix is to circle the highest loading in a test or item vector. An item may then be assigned to the factor in which it has the highest loading. This procedure will guarantee that an item is not assigned to more than one cluster. It will not, however, guarantee that all factors will have items assigned to them nor will it guarantee the assignment of an approximately equal number of items to each of the factors.

One of the difficulties of this method is that certain items may be assigned to a factor even though they have loadings in it which are lower than those of some items that have been circled for another factor. This inconsistency may be circumvented by specifying that no item with a circled loading in a factor column shall be included in the set if there are uncircled factor loadings in that column higher than the circled loadings. One would identify the highest uncircled loading in a vector of factor loadings and then eliminate from the set all items that had circled loadings in the factor less than this value. Such a procedure can, of course, result in the elimination of many items from the set.

RESULTS

Attempts to use the clustering rationale based on the simple structure factor matrix typically give an uneven distribution of item allocations. Thus it is not a satisfactory method for clustering items into scales so that enough items to yield reasonably reliable scores are assigned to all scales. If factors that do not have enough items in them are eliminated, then one must also discard the items assigned to them or decide in which scales to put these items. The procedure of eliminating circled items when higher uncircled values occur in the same factor eliminates even more items. It is seen then that this strategy of clustering can waste many items that may be useful in a multidimensional factor scale.

Another result characteristic of this method is similar to one indicated for the multiple group method. If we calculate factor scores simply as the sum of items positively responded to for each scale and calculate a correlation matrix of these factor scores, undesirably high correlations among the factor scores typically result. At best, therefore, only a rough approximation to primary factor dimensions is achieved.

In general, the clustering methods have not given satisfactory results. The moral to be learned from such analyses is that the kinds of multiple personality scales based simply on the segregation of subsets of items for each factor do not give sufficiently independent factor scores.

MATRIX PARTITIONING AND SUPERMATRIX CONSTRUCTION

We have seen that a number of methods are available for handling the factor analysis of very large data matrices on currently available computer installations. We have also seen that these present disadvantages, both as to time requirements and adequacy of solutions. A method (Horst, 1966b) that overcomes some of these disadvantages consists of the successive partitioning of matrices and construction of supermatrices on the basis of certain rationally specified computational procedures. The method is similar to the one discussed under "Successive Elimination of Data Vectors" in that one partitions a large data matrix into submatrices and performs operations on each of these to get a new set of submatrices. These are then combined into a supermatrix whose smaller simple order is much less than that of the original data matrix. Again, a partitioning takes place and operations proceed on each of the submatrices to yield matrices of order smaller than the submatrices. This succession of matrix partitioning and supermatrix construction proceeds until no further partitioning is required. The method is different from Tryon's method discussed earlier in the chapter in that it tends to preserve more of the information in the original data matrix as the successive reductions take place. We shall here consider the method in terms of the rationale, the tape requirements, and the time requirements.

RATIONALE

The rationale of this method is based on the assumptions of the simple structure type factor analysis developed by Thurstone (1947). The simple structure concept, we recall, assumes that the factor loadings should be relatively invariant, irrespective of the particular samples of cases and variables on which the analyses are based. Obviously, of course, if one set of variables includes none of the factors in another set, no method of analysis can yield the same factors from both, but if there is overlapping in the factors represented by two different sets of variables, then one may expect with the use of adequate simple structure methods that the overlapping factors will emerge in independent analyses as recognizably the same factors.

Also, one cannot expect factors to emerge if there is no variation with respect to those factors in a particular sample. However, if there is variation with respect to the factors, then even though this variation may itself differ greatly from one sample of cases to another, the simple structure types of analysis should tend to reveal the same factors from one group to another.

The rationale of the method begins then with some arbitrary partitioning of the data matrix, either by variables or entities. The smaller order of the submatrices may be from sixty to 100. This smaller order is determined by the size of a matrix whose minor product moment can be conveniently handled within core.

If one starts with a partitioning by entities, this implies an obverse factor analysis on each of the submatrices to get a factor loading matrix. One then constructs a supermatrix of these factor matrices, placing them side by side, and repartitions the supermatrix into subsets of width from sixty to 100. These are then separately analyzed to a prespecified number of factors, and the submatrices of factor loading vectors are put into a supermatrix. The routine is continued until the final factor loading matrix has been calculated.

In the alternative procedure, successive sets of factor score matrices are calculated by the strategy of partitioning first by variables. These factor score matrices are scaled according to the corresponding basic diagonal elements. The partitioning, basic structure analysis, and supermatrix construction proceeds with these weighted factor score submatrices until the final factor score matrix is arrived at. Then using this factor score matrix, the solution for the factor loading matrix can be obtained from the original data matrix by well-known methods (Horst, 1963, 1965).

TAPE REQUIREMENTS

The peripheral storage unit requirements for this procedure are no more than the maximum requirements indicated in the procedures outlined in preceding sections. Ordinarily a maximum of five units will be adequate for the complete solution which carries through to the scoring matrix and the correlations of the factor scores.

TIME AND ACCURACY

The time requirements for this procedure are from one third to one fifth of those outlined in the first and second sections of this chapter. A comparison of the results from this procedure with others obtained by more exact methods suggests that the loss of accuracy is negligible compared to the inaccuracy of typical experimental data matrices.

DIRECT VARIMAX SOLUTIONS

The possibility of evading the principal axis factor solution and getting the varimax solution directly from either the correlation or the data matrix might be tempting. Methods for achieving this are available (Horst, 1965). It may be thought that by avoiding the laborious principal axis solution one may save much time, but experience indicates that in general more iterations are required for satisfactory stabilization to interpretable results when the varimax factors are derived directly from the correlation matrix than if they come via the principal axis matrix. It has been shown (Horst, 1962) that we need not be too much concerned about the accuracy of a particular principal axis factor vector if its corresponding eigenvalue or basic diagonal is very close to the one which is next highest. It is doubtful then that the direct varimax solution, even though it does avoid the principal axis solution, is faster than varimax solutions based on the principal axis solution.

CHAPTER **10**

Experimental Applications

7he method for matrix partitioning and supermatrix construction discussed in Chapter 9 was applied to data collected by Campbell (1959) with a questionnaire developed by her for a Ph.D. thesis. This research was conducted under the author's supervision when only the IBM 650 computer was available for the analyses. Approximation procedures developed earlier by the author for estimating the factor structure of a large number of variables were used by Campbell. More recently, newer methods (Horst, 1966b), which have been referred to in previous chapters, have been applied to Campbell's data. Some of the results obtained by these newer methods are reported for illustrative purposes in this chapter.

Campbell (1959) developed an inventory of items designed

to measure twenty-four of Murray's (1938) postulated needs. The subject was required to check one of five responses, numbered from 1 to 5, to indicate how he compared with other people with respect to each item. A subject's score on an item was taken to be the number of the response he marked. The group consisted of 211 college students. The inventory was given twice to the subjects with an interval of a week between the two administrations. The factor analyses are based on both administrations. Each person's first and second administration item scores are treated as though they were from two separate persons. The rigidly formal mathematical statistician may object to this procedure, but we cannot emphasize too strongly that his models are not appropriate or adequate for many factor analysis procedures and for this one in particular.

In this chapter we shall present results from the principal axis factor solution, the simple structure regression solution, the integer response-weight scoring results, and the T-score factor measures.

PRINCIPAL AXIS FACTOR SOLUTION

The first step in the preparation of factor scales from a set of personality items is ideally a principal axis solution of the item variables. For a large number of variables or items, readily available computer facilities require special procedures (Horst, 1966b). We shall consider in this section the parameters of the solution, the sets of eigenvalues or basic diagonals, the principal axis matrix, and comparison of the first principal axis and item means.

PARAMETERS OF THE SOLUTION

One of the first decisions to be made in using the methods referred to in previous chapters is whether the data matrix of item scores shall be partitioned by rows or columns, that is, by persons or test items. Other things being equal, it is probably best theoretically to partition by rows rather than columns. The total number of rows in the data matrix for Campbell's (1959) data is 422, or twice the number of cases. The total number of items is 288. In any case, we probably would partition by rows in this study since the number of rows is not twice the number of columns.

We take sixty for the maximum smaller order of a submatrix and ninety for the maximum smaller order of the final matrix. We take twenty for the maximum number of factors for submatrices, seventeen for the maximum number of factors for the final matrix, and twenty for the maximum number of iterations for any factor. The tolerance limit for successive approximations to an eigenvalue is .0001. The maximum proportion of total variance accounted for by the principal axis factors extracted is .75. Variations of some of these parameters have been tried (Horst, 1966b) and the results do not differ greatly from those given in this chapter.

EIGENVALUES

It is of interest to note the sets of eigenvalues or basic diagonals of the successive product moment matrices corresponding to the submatrices of the partitioned matrices for each of the successive cycles of matrix partitioning and supermatrix construction. Table 1 presents these eigenvalues, together with the number of iterations taken for each. It will be recalled that the maximum number of iterations is twenty. Each block within the table gives, in the first column, the eigenvalues or variance accounted for by the corresponding factor, and in the second the corresponding number of iterations. Blocks 1-1 to 1-8 are for the first ten factors of the first cycle of operations. There are eight of these blocks because the number of entities, 422, divided by 160, the maximum number of submatrix rows, is 7+, hence 8, since each fraction is counted as 1. Blocks 2-1 through 2-3 are for the first ten factors of the second cycle of operations. Block 3-1 is for the final matrix.

PRINCIPAL AXIS MATRIX

The final principal axis matrix for the first twenty of the 288 item variables and the first ten of the seventeen factors is given in Table 2. Each element in the second column in this table is the sum of squares of elements of the corresponding seventeen factors. The remaining ten columns give the first ten of the seventeen prin-

Experimental Applications

Table 1. Eigenvalues of Submatrix Product Moments, with Number of Iterations

1 – 1		1 – 2		1 – 3		1 – 4	
7.944	9	5.682	12	5.638	11	6.256	8
3.866	20	3.633	20	3.279	12	2.704	20
3.349	16	3.208	11	2.484	20	2.845	10
2.558	19	2.119	20	2.140	15	1.493	20
2.231	14	1.944	14	1.800	20	1.632	20
1.633	20	1.578	20	1.735	16	1.301	18
1.446	15	1.523	20	1.421	20	1.142	20
1.249	18	1.236	20	1.229	20	1.086	20
1.092	20	1.094	20	1.043	20	1.098	20
1.004	20	1.028	20	0.999	20	1.034	20

1 – 5		1 – 6		1 – 7		1 – 8	
3.902	20	7.025	7	4.882	15	3.630	20
2.909	20	4.578	20	2.893	20	3.440	9
2.493	10	2.784	10	2.535	10	2.452	20
1.683	20	1.674	20	1.968	18	1.764	15
1.447	20	1.756	20	1.397	20	1.502	20
1.580	20	1.571	20	1.288	17	1.326	15
1.336	20	1.304	20	1.089	20	1.168	20
1.153	20	1.121	20	1.077	20	0.911	20
1.042	20	1.236	20	0.980	20	0.813	20
1.020	20	0.959	20	0.830	20	0.736	20

2 – 1		2 – 2		2 – 3		3 – 1	
15.464	6	12.569	10	7.388	11	31.302	5
7.968	8	7.806	17	5.022	20	17.129	20
6.460	15	5.506	19	4.350	12	14.633	11
4.473	20	4.501	18	3.739	19	9.624	17
3.436	20	3.755	12	2.805	17	7.891	16
3.140	20	2.359	18	2.228	20	6.602	20
3.132	20	2.086	20	2.128	20	5.507	20
2.673	20	1.936	20	1.758	20	4.776	20
2.558	20	1.714	20	1.700	20	4.332	20
2.126	20	1.608	20	1.683	20	3.979	20

Table 2. Principal Axis Matrix

Item	Com.	1	2	3	4	5	6	7	8	9	10
1	0.32	0.1	0.2	−0.1	0.2	0.0	0.3	0.1	0.1	−0.0	−0.0
2	0.38	0.3	−0.1	0.2	0.0	0.0	−0.3	−0.0	0.0	−0.1	−0.1
3	0.56	0.5	−0.3	−0.4	0.1	−0.1	−0.1	−0.1	−0.2	−0.0	0.0
4	0.35	−0.1	−0.4	0.0	−0.2	−0.2	−0.1	0.1	0.0	0.0	−0.0
5	0.39	−0.2	−0.2	0.3	0.1	0.2	0.0	−0.3	0.0	0.1	−0.1
6	0.44	0.5	−0.1	0.2	0.1	−0.1	0.0	−0.2	0.0	−0.2	0.0
7	0.57	0.4	−0.4	0.3	0.2	−0.1	0.1	0.1	−0.2	−0.2	0.1
8	0.38	0.3	0.2	−0.0	−0.1	0.0	−0.1	0.1	−0.1	−0.0	0.1
9	0.53	0.2	0.3	0.2	−0.4	−0.1	0.1	0.0	0.1	−0.0	0.2
10	0.17	−0.1	−0.2	0.0	−0.2	0.0	−0.1	−0.1	0.1	0.1	−0.1
11	0.49	0.3	−0.0	−0.1	−0.1	0.2	0.1	0.2	0.0	−0.2	0.2
12	0.60	0.5	−0.1	0.1	0.1	−0.3	0.1	−0.1	−0.0	−0.4	0.1
13	0.16	0.1	0.0	0.2	−0.2	−0.1	0.1	0.0	0.0	0.1	0.0
14	0.49	0.3	0.4	0.2	−0.2	−0.1	0.1	0.0	−0.1	0.0	−0.2
15	0.42	0.4	−0.2	−0.2	−0.3	−0.0	−0.1	−0.2	−0.0	0.1	−0.2
16	0.37	0.2	−0.1	0.3	−0.1	0.3	−0.0	0.1	0.1	−0.1	−0.0
17	0.32	−0.2	−0.0	−0.2	−0.3	0.1	−0.2	0.1	−0.1	0.0	−0.0
18	0.38	0.4	0.2	−0.1	0.2	0.0	0.1	0.1	0.0	0.2	0.0
19	0.54	0.2	0.4	0.1	−0.2	−0.1	0.2	−0.0	−0.3	0.1	−0.3
20	0.39	0.1	−0.3	0.1	−0.4	−0.1	−0.1	0.1	0.0	−0.1	−0.1

cipal axis factor loading vectors. The loadings are given only to one decimal place. This seems adequate, considering the accuracy of the data.

COMPARISON OF FIRST PRINCIPAL AXIS AND ITEM MEANS

The most interesting of the principal axis factor loadings is the first. If its elements are plotted against the means of the items for the first administration of the items, we get a scatter diagram as in Table 3. Here we see a definite positive relationship which supports Edward's (1964) observations (see Chapter 6). Suppose, however, we reverse the scoring of all the items with negative first principal axis factor loadings and recalculate their means. Then these loadings become positive. If now we plot the means against the factor loadings, we get a scatter plot as in Table 4. Here the correlation between factor loadings and means is obviously negligible. It appears that with the use of the comparative response options and sign reversals, the social desirability factor has been greatly reduced if not eliminated.

SIMPLE STRUCTURE REGRESSION SOLUTION

To get a matrix of scoring weights that will give, from the raw item scores, uncorrelated standardized simple structure scores, we first get a simple structure factor loading matrix and then a matrix of regression weights.

SIMPLE STRUCTURE FACTOR MATRIX

From the principal axis factor matrix we get, by means of a square orthonormal transformation, a factor loading matrix that satisfies the varimax criterion of Kaiser (1958). For the development of the factor score scoring matrix, we do not actually need the simple structure factor matrix but only the principal axis factor matrix and the varimax transformation matrix. However, for labeling purposes we do need the simple structure factor loading matrix. From this matrix we can group items with high loadings in a factor and attempt to give a name to what the items have in common.

Table 3. Relation between Item Means and First Principal Axis Factor Loadings

			Item Means × 10																		
	20	21	22	23	24	25	26	27	28	29	30	31	32	33	34	35	36	37	38	39	40
8																					
7																					
6																		1			
5																3	2	1	1		
4					2		1	6	1	1	3	5	5	4	3	4	2				
3					1	2	2	3	2	4	4	7	10	8	5	3		3			
2					1	2	2	2	2	3	7	6	8	6	2	1					
1						4	4	4	4	5	3	4	3	2	4						
0	1	1			1	3	1	2	3	9	2	2	2	2	2	1					
−1	1	1		1	2	3	3	3	3	2	2	1	2								
−2				1	3	1	1	2	2	3	4	1	2	2							
−3					1		5		5	1	3	1									
−4						1	1	4													
−5																					
−6																					
−7																					
−8																					

First Principal Axis Factor Loadings × 10

194

Table 4. Relation between Reflected Item Means and First Principal Axis Factor Loadings

Reflected Factor Loadings	Reflected Means																				
	20	21	22	23	24	25	26	27	28	29	30	31	32	33	34	35	36	37	38	39	40
8	1																				
7												1	2	2							
6					2		1	6		1	3	5	5	4	7	3	1	1			
5					1	2	2	3	1	4	4	7	10	8	9	4	3	2	1		
3					1	4	2	4	2	3	7	7	13	6	3	3	3	1			
4					1	3	2	4	2	2	6	6	5	4	9	1	3	4			
2							1	2	6	5	7	5	5	5	3	4	2				1
1									5	10	4	1	2								
0										2											

As we recall, the primary objective here is to facilitate communication and not to discover "real" factors.

Table 5 gives the simple structure factor loadings for the first twenty items and ten factors. The actual loadings have been multiplied by 100 and rounded to the nearest whole number. This table provides the basis for the item groupings on the basis of which labels may be established. The first column after the item numbers in the table indicates the sign of each item. Those with negative signs should be interpreted in the reverse direction.

RAW SCORE REGRESSION MATRIX

The general inverse of the varimax factor loading matrix when multiplied into the standardized data matrix yields a matrix of standardized simple structure factor scores. These scores are mutually orthogonal in the sample to within the degree of accuracy permitted by the computational procedures. Ordinarily, however, one would have raw item scores rather than standardized scores from which to calculate the factor scores. It is therefore necessary to scale the general inverse of the simple structure factor matrix by the reciprocal of the item standard deviations and to calculate an appropriate vector of constants—one for each factor.

Table 6 gives the first twenty rows and the first ten of seventeen columns of the matrix of regression weights by which the raw score item data matrix is multiplied to give standard score simple structure factor scores. Only the first decimal is retained, as these weights are not recommended for use in actually computing factor scores. The practical procedure recommended is indicated below, under "The *T*-Score Factor Scales." The last row of Table 6 gives the vector of additive constants for the first ten factors required to yield factor scores with zero means for the sample.

INTEGER RESPONSE-WEIGHT SCORING RESULTS

If the factor scores are to be obtained by hand scoring, then the regression scoring matrix is not practical. However, we may obtain varying degrees of accuracy simply by constructing scoring

Table 5. Simple Structure Factor Matrix

Item	Sign	1	2	3	4	5	6	7	8	9	10
1	1.	-8	1	-9	27	11	31	-0	5	4	5
2	1.	13	31	5	-10	-20	2	7	-4	24	-17
3	1.	65	-8	3	0	9	-9	17	10	15	-6
4	-1.	9	20	9	33	5	1	-29	7	-11	2
5	-1.	18	11	-22	11	14	-2	2	-5	2	18
6	1.	28	15	18	3	4	-3	-1	-4	43	6
7	1.	13	0	46	-1	4	-1	25	-12	45	3
8	1.	20	26	-0	-5	12	11	-5	-3	0	18
9	1.	-6	20	-0	-8	-2	4	-11	8	9	65
10	-1.	4	8	11	18	12	0	-2	1	4	6
11	1.	28	7	17	-5	-4	-6	1	6	5	0
12	1.	22	5	14	9	13	-1	3	9	67	10
13	1.	-9	5	10	-5	7	5	8	-2	4	23
14	1.	6	57	-6	2	12	-2	-9	-3	-3	24
15	1.	38	3	-3	-19	11	9	10	19	16	11
16	1.	2	25	18	-11	-22	9	5	-10	14	-7
17	-1.	3	16	7	23	-12	-13	5	-15	26	-8
18	1.	32	11	3	35	17	19	3	-13	2	3
19	1.	12	25	3	-3	14	2	-20	-11	-5	57
20	-1.	0	-1	-4	45	3	2	-12	-3	-22	1

Table 6. Raw Score Regression Matrix

	1	2	3	4	5	6	7	8	9	10
1	−0.5	−0.1	−0.5	0.3	0.1	1.5	0.2	0.4	0.5	0.1
2	0.1	0.6	−0.3	−0.3	−0.5	0.5	−0.2	−0.2	0.4	−0.7
3	0.5	−0.2	0.1	−0.0	0.1	−0.3	−0.0	0.2	−0.0	0.0
4	−0.1	−0.0	−0.2	−0.3	−0.1	0.1	0.5	−0.1	0.1	0.1
5	0.0	0.1	0.1	−0.2	−0.1	0.0	−0.1	0.2	−0.0	−0.2
6	0.2	−0.0	−0.0	−0.0	−0.1	−0.1	−0.4	0.0	0.6	0.1
7	0.0	−0.2	0.5	0.1	0.1	−0.1	0.0	−0.2	0.4	0.2
8	0.2	0.1	−0.0	−0.3	0.1	0.4	−0.1	−0.2	−0.0	0.3
9	−0.1	−0.2	−0.1	−0.1	−0.5	0.0	0.1	0.5	0.1	1.3
10	0.1	0.1	−0.3	−0.2	−0.3	−0.0	−0.1	−0.1	−0.1	−0.1
11	0.1	−0.2	0.5	0.0	−0.2	−0.6	0.1	0.2	−0.1	0.0
12	−0.1	−0.3	−0.0	0.1	0.0	0.1	−0.3	0.5	1.0	0.1
13	−0.3	−0.1	0.2	0.2	0.1	0.0	0.4	0.1	−0.1	0.5
14	0.1	0.8	−0.1	−0.2	0.2	−0.0	−0.0	−0.2	−0.3	0.0
15	0.2	−0.0	−0.1	−0.1	0.2	0.1	0.2	0.6	0.0	0.1
16	−0.1	0.1	−0.0	−0.1	−0.5	0.2	0.1	−0.1	0.2	−0.2
17	−0.1	−0.2	0.0	−0.2	0.4	0.2	0.1	0.4	−0.4	0.3
18	0.3	−0.1	0.1	0.5	0.3	0.5	0.1	−0.6	−0.1	−0.1
19	0.2	0.0	0.1	−0.3	0.0	−0.0	−0.3	−0.3	−0.2	0.8
20	−0.1	0.1	−0.1	−0.5	−0.0	−0.1	0.1	0.2	0.2	−0.1
	41.5	−10.2	27.8	138.1	12.2	−65.9	26.3	94.9	28.3	24.2

stencils that require only counting of responses for each stencil and multiplication of frequencies by numbers not greater than nine. For each factor, sets of stencils may be prepared. The number of sets for each factor depends on the highest response scoring weight it is desired to use. The higher this number, the greater the number of stencils required, but the greater also will be the accuracy achieved. As examples we shall present the first twenty rows and first ten columns of tables of integer scoring weights from which stencils may be produced, and tables of factor score correlations for the various maximum weights.

INTEGER WEIGHT SCORING MATRICES

The maximum integer weights which have been tried are 1, 2, 3, 5, and 9. Table 7 gives the first twenty rows of scoring weights for each response element for each of the first ten factors for each item, for the maximum weight of 1. For each element there are five digits. (Where only one zero occurs in an element, it is to be interpreted as having five zero digits.) The digit to the left applies to the lowest response category and the one to the right to the highest, that is, "much less than" and "much more than," respectively. It will be noted that not all items are included. This is because for some items all weights for responses of all factors were zero. It will also be noted that for all response set digits, at least one of the extreme digits is zero. For those with a nonzero digit on the left, the item is automatically scored positively for the factor. For those with nonzero digits on the right, the scoring of the item is automatically reversed. Since there are only 1's and 0's in the table, only one set of stencils is required for each factor. The score is simply the number of responses checked in "1" positions for each factor.

Table 8 gives the first twenty rows and first ten columns of the response element scoring integers for a maximum integer of 2. The interpretation of these weights is the same as for the maximum integer of 1. It will be noted now, however, that no items among the first twenty have been omitted, since for every item at least one response element for at least one factor has a weight of at least 1.

Table 7. Integer Response Weight Scoring Matrix, Maximum 1

	1	2	3	4	5	6	7	8	9	10
1	11	0	0	0	0	11000	0	0	0	0
2	0	10000	0	0	0	0	0	0	0	1
3	11000	0	0	0	0	0	0	0	0	0
6	0	0	0	0	0	0	0	0	0	0
8	0	0	0	0	0	0	0	0	0	0
9	0	0	0	0	0	0	0	0	0	11000
11	0	0	0	0	0	0	0	0	0	0
12	0	11000	0	0	0	0	0	0	0	0
14	0	0	0	0	0	0	0	0	11000	0
16	0	0	0	0	0	0	0	0	0	0
17	0	0	0	0	0	0	0	0	0	10000
19	0	0	0	0	0	0	0	0	0	0
20	11	0	0	0	0	10000	0	0	0	0
21	0	10000	0	0	0	0	0	0	0	0
24	0	0	0	0	0	0	0	0	0	0
25	0	0	0	0	0	0	0	0	10000	0
26	0	0	0	0	0	0	0	0	0	0
29	0	0	0	0	0	0	0	0	0	0
30	0	0	0	0	0	0	0	0	0	0
32	10000	0	0	0	0	0	0	0	0	0

Table 8. Integer Response Weight Scoring Matrix, Maximum 2

	1	2	3	4	5	6	7	8	9	10
1	112	0	11	10000	0	21100	0	10000	11000	0
2	0	11100	0	1	1	11000	0	0	10000	111
3	21100	0	0	0	0	0	11000	0	0	0
4	0	0	0	1	0	0	0	0	0	0
5	0	0	11000	0	0	0	1	0	11000	0
6	11000	0	0	0	0	0	0	0	10000	0
7	0	0	0	1	0	10000	0	10000	0	0
8	10000	0	1	0	11	0	0	0	0	21100
9	0	0	11000	0	0	0	0	0	0	0
10	0	0	0	0	0	0	0	0	21100	0
11	0	0	0	0	11	11	0	10000	0	11000
12	0	1	0	0	0	0	0	0	1	0
13	11	0	0	0	1	0	0	11000	0	0
14	0	11100	0	0	11	0	0	0	0	0
15	0	0	0	0	10000	0	0	10000	1	0
16	0	0	0	11000	0	11000	0	11	0	0
17	0	0	0	1	0	0	0	0	0	0
18	11000	0	0	11	0	0	0	0	0	11100
19	10000	0	0	0	0	0	0	0	0	0
20	0	0	0	0	0	0	0	0	0	0

Strictly speaking, we require two sets of scoring stencils for each factor, one set for counting the 1-weight responses checked and the other for counting the 2-weight responses checked. However, since the percentage checking the extreme position is so small, no serious reduction in accuracy would occur if all extreme locations were assigned the same digit as the response element immediately adjacent. Inspection of the tables shows that no response weights would then be greater than 1. In this case, a single set of scoring stencils could be used as in the case of a maximum of 1. Again the score for a factor is simply the number of marks appearing for the 1-weight responses.

Table 9 has the same meaning as the previous table, except now the maximum weight is 3. Here one would normally have three sets of stencils for each factor. The score for a factor would be 1 times the 1-weight response checks, plus 2 times the 2-weight response checks, plus 3 times the 3-weight response checks. Here again, we could assign the same weight to extreme responses as to weights for the adjacent responses and thus reduce the sets of scoring stencils for each factor to two.

Tables 10 and 11 have the same interpretation for maximum weights of 5 and 9, respectively, as in the previous cases. Here again, one may reduce the sets of scoring stencils by one by assigning to the extreme responses the weights of the adjacent responses.

FACTOR SCORE CORRELATIONS

For each of the maximum integer scoring procedures it is possible (Horst, 1966b) to find the factor score correlations among the scales for each administration separately and for the first administration with the second. These three tables are presented for each of the maximum integer response weights considered in the preceding section.

Table 12 consists of three submatrices for the maximum integer weight of 1. The first submatrix gives the correlations among the first ten factor scores for the first administration. The second submatrix gives the correlations of the first administration with the second. The third gives the correlations among the factor scores for

Table 9. Integer Response Weight Scoring Matrix, Maximum 3

	1	2	3	4	5	6	7	8	9	10
1	1122	0	111	11000	0	32110	0	11000	11100	0
2	0	21100	1	11	11	11100	0	0	11000	112
3	22110	0	0	0	0	1	11100	0	0	0
4	1	0	1	11	0	0	0	0	0	0
5	0	0	0	0	0	0	11	0	0	0
6	11100	0	11100	0	111	0	0	0	11100	0
7	0	1	0	11	11	11000	0	0	11000	0
8	11000	0	0	0	0	0	0	11000	0	10000
9	1	0	0	1	0	0	0	0	0	32110
10	0	0	11	0	0	111	11	0	0	0
11	0	1	11100	0	0	0	0	11000	22110	0
12	0	11	0	0	0	0	11000	0	0	0
13	111	0	10000	0	0	0	0	0	11	11100
14	10000	22110	0	0	0	0	0	0	0	0
15	11000	0	0	0	111	0	0	11100	0	0
16	0	0	0	0	11000	0	0	0	11	0
17	0	0	0	1	10000	11100	0	11000	0	10000
18	11100	0	0	11100	0	0	0	0	11	0
19	11000	0	0	11	0	0	1	111	0	21100
20	1	0	0	111	0	0	0	0	10000	0

Table 10. Integer Response Weight Scoring Matrix, Maximum 5

	1	2	3	4	5	6	7	8	9	10
1	1234	1	112	11100	0	54210	11000	11100	21100	0
2	10000	32110	111	111	112	21100	1	0	11100	1123
3	43210	11	0	0	0	111	0	10000	0	0
4	111	0	11	111	1	0	21100	11000	0	10000
5	0	0	10000	11	0	0	0	0	0	11
6	21100	0	0	0	0	0	112	1	22110	0
7	0	11	22110	0	10000	0	0	1	11100	10000
8	11100	0	0	111	112	0	0	0	0	11100
9	11	11	0	0	111	21100	0	21100	10000	54210
10	10000	10000	111	11	1	0	0	0	0	0
11	11000	11	22110	0	0	1122	0	11000	0	0
12	11	111	0	0	0	0	111	21100	43210	0
13	112	1	11000	10000	0	0	11100	0	1	21100
14	11000	33210	0	10000	10000	0	0	1	111	0
15	11100	0	0	11	11000	0	10000	22110	0	10000
16	1	0	0	0	112	11000	0	0	11000	1
17	1	11	0	0	11100	11000	0	11100	112	11000
18	22110	1	0	22110	11000	21100	0	112	0	0
19	21100	0	0	111	0	0	111	111	11	32210
20	11	10000	0	112	0	1	0	11000	11000	0

Table 11. Integer Response Weight Scoring Matrix, Maximum 9

	1	2	3	4	5	6	7	8	9	10
1	2457	111	1234	32110	0	97420	11100	32110	33210	0
2	11000	54210	112	1122	1123	32210	111	11	22110	1235
3	75420	111	10000	0	0	112	0	11100	0	0
4	112	0	112	1122	11	10000	32210	11	11000	11000
5	0	10000	11000	111	1	0	11	11100	0	111
6	32210	0	43210	0	0	11	1123	0	43210	0
7	0	112	0	0	0	0	0	11	32110	11100
8	32110	10000	1	10000	11000	32110	1	111	0	21100
9	112	111	1122	1122	1223	0	11000	32210	11100	97420
10	11000	11000	43210	0	1122	0	11000	0	11	0
11	11100	112	0	112	111	1234	1	11100	0	0
12	111	1122	1122	0	0	0	1122	32210	75420	11000
13	1233	11	43210	11000	11000	0	22110	10000	111	32210
14	21100	65320	0	11100	11100	0	0	11	1122	0
15	22110	0	21100	111	11100	0	11100	43210	0	11000
16	111	11000	11	1	1223	11000	10000	11	11100	111
17	111	111	1	0	22110	11100	10000	22110	1123	21100
18	43210	111	0	112	21100	11100	0	1223	11	0
19	32110	0	11000	1122	0	32210	112	112	112	64310
20	112	11100	0	1233	0	11	11000	11100	21100	0

205

Table 12. Factor Score Correlations, Maximum 1

First Administration

1	2	3	4	5	6	7	8	9	10
1.0	0.2	0.2	0.2	0.4	0.4	0.4	0.2	0.3	0.2
0.2	1.0	0.3	0.2	0.2	0.3	0.1	—0.0	0.3	0.5
0.2	0.3	1.0	0.2	0.3	0.3	0.4	0.0	0.4	0.1
0.2	0.2	0.2	1.0	0.2	0.3	0.0	0.2	0.2	0.1
0.4	0.2	0.3	0.2	1.0	0.4	0.2	0.1	0.2	0.3
0.4	0.3	0.3	0.3	0.4	1.0	0.3	0.1	0.3	0.3
0.4	0.1	0.4	0.0	0.2	0.3	1.0	—0.0	0.3	0.0
0.2	—0.0	0.0	0.2	0.1	0.1	—0.0	1.0	0.0	0.0
0.3	0.3	0.4	0.2	0.2	0.3	0.3	0.0	1.0	—0.0
0.2	0.5	0.1	0.1	0.3	0.3	0.0	—0.0	0.3	1.0

First Administration with Second Administration

1	2	3	4	5	6	7	8	9	10
0.9	0.1	0.2	0.2	0.3	0.4	0.3	0.3	0.2	0.1
0.2	0.9	0.2	0.2	0.3	0.3	0.1	0.0	0.3	0.5
0.2	0.2	0.8	0.1	0.2	0.3	0.4	0.0	0.4	0.1

0.2	0.4	0.4	0.4	0.2	0.3	0.2
0.2	0.2	0.3	0.1	—0.0	0.3	0.4
0.1	0.2	0.2	0.4	—0.1	0.3	0.1
0.7	0.2	0.3	0.1	0.2	0.1	0.1
0.2	0.7	0.4	0.1	0.0	0.2	0.3
0.3	0.3	0.7	0.3	0.1	0.3	0.2
0.0	0.1	0.2	0.9	—0.0	0.3	0.0
0.2	0.2	0.2	0.1	0.7	—0.0	0.0
0.1	0.2	0.2	0.2	—0.0	0.8	0.2
0.0	0.2	0.2	—0.0	—0.0	0.2	0.9

Second Administration

1.0	0.2	0.2	0.2	0.2	0.4	0.5	0.4	0.4	0.3
0.2	1.0	0.2	0.2	0.3	0.3	0.1	0.1	0.4	0.5
0.2	0.2	1.0	0.2	0.3	0.4	0.4	0.0	0.4	0.1
0.2	0.2	0.2	1.0	0.2	0.3	0.1	0.2	0.1	0.1
0.4	0.3	0.3	0.2	1.0	0.4	0.2	0.3	0.3	0.3
0.5	0.3	0.4	0.3	0.4	1.0	0.4	0.2	0.3	0.2
0.4	0.1	0.4	0.1	0.2	0.4	1.0	0.1	0.3	0.0
0.4	0.1	0.0	0.2	0.3	0.2	0.1	1.0	0.0	0.0
0.3	0.4	0.4	0.1	0.3	0.3	0.3	0.0	1.0	0.2
0.2	0.5	0.1	0.1	0.3	0.2	0.0	0.0	0.2	1.0

Table 13. Factor Score Correlations, Maximum 2

	1	2	3	4	5	6	7	8	9	10
First Administration										
	1.0	0.1	0.2	0.0	0.0	0.1	0.1	0.1	0.2	—0.1
	0.1	1.0	0.2	0.1	0.2	0.1	0.1	0.1	0.3	0.2
	0.2	0.2	1.0	0.2	0.2	0.2	0.2	0.2	0.4	0.1
	0.0	0.1	0.2	1.0	0.2	0.1	0.1	0.3	0.2	0.2
	0.0	0.2	0.2	0.2	1.0	0.1	—0.1	0.0	0.1	0.0
	0.1	0.1	0.2	0.1	0.1	1.0	0.1	0.2	0.3	—0.0
	0.1	0.1	0.2	0.1	—0.1	0.1	1.0	0.0	0.2	—0.0
	0.1	0.1	0.2	0.3	0.0	0.2	0.0	1.0	0.0	0.1
	0.2	0.3	0.4	0.2	0.1	0.3	0.2	0.0	1.0	0.1
	—0.1	0.2	0.1	0.2	0.0	—0.0	—0.0	0.1	0.1	1.0
First Administration with Second Administration										
	0.9	0.0	0.1	—0.1	0.1	0.1	0.1	—0.0	0.2	—0.1
	0.1	0.9	0.2	0.2	0.2	0.1	0.1	0.2	0.3	0.2
	0.1	0.1	0.7	0.2	0.2	0.2	0.2	0.2	0.4	0.1
	0.0	0.2	0.2	0.8	0.2	0.1	0.1	0.2	0.1	0.1

Second Administration

0.0	0.1	0.1	0.2	0.2	0.7	0.1	—0.1	0.1	0.1
0.2	0.1	0.1	0.3	0.1	0.1	0.7	0.1	0.1	—0.0
0.2	0.1	0.1	0.3	0.1	—0.0	0.2	0.9	0.2	—0.0
0.0	0.1	0.1	0.2	0.2	0.1	0.1	0.0	0.6	—0.0
0.2	0.2	0.2	0.3	0.2	0.1	0.2	0.0	0.1	0.0
—0.1	0.1	0.2	0.1	0.2	—0.0	—0.1	—0.0	0.1	0.8

1.0	0.1	0.2	—0.0	0.1	0.2	0.2	0.2	0.0	—0.0
0.1	1.0	0.1	0.2	0.1	0.0	0.2	0.1	0.3	0.2
0.2	0.1	1.0	0.2	0.4	0.4	0.3	0.5	0.4	0.2
—0.0	0.2	0.2	1.0	0.2	0.1	0.1	0.2	0.1	0.2
0.1	0.2	0.1	0.2	1.0	0.3	—0.0	0.3	0.2	0.1
0.2	0.1	—0.1	0.3	0.3	1.0	0.2	0.3	0.3	—0.1
0.2	0.1	—0.0	0.3	0.2	0.2	1.0	0.2	0.3	—0.0
0.2	0.2	0.1	0.5	0.3	0.3	0.2	1.0	0.3	0.1
0.0	0.1	0.1	0.4	0.3	0.3	1.0	0.3	1.0	0.1
0.3	0.2	1.0	0.2	0.1	—0.1	0.1	0.1	0.1	1.0

the second administration. It will be noted that there are many correlations of .3 or greater in all three submatrices, therefore we do not get as much independence among the factors as is desirable for factor scores. The diagonals of the middle submatrix are actually retest reliability coefficients. These range from .7 to .9 in the first decimal. The factors with reliability .7 and above are doubtless satisfactorily high.

Table 13 gives the same data for the maximum weight of 2. The correlations tend to be slightly lower and would doubtless be satisfactory. If only unit-weight stencils were used, the scoring would not be laborious. The reliabilities, aside from factor 8, are all .7 or better.

Table 14 is for a maximum weight of 3 and has lower correlations than the previous two. The reliabilities are all satisfactory. If all 3-weights were reduced to 2, only two sets of scoring stencils would be required for each factor and the scoring would not be difficult for a limited number of cases.

Table 15 is for a maximum weight of 5. Only a minority of the correlations are greater than .2. The reliabilities are adequate. By a reduction to four sets of scoring stencils, the scoring would not be prohibitive and the results would be quite satisfactory both for reliability and independence of scales.

Table 16 is for a maximum weight of 9. As can be seen, the results are highly satisfactory, both for reliability and independence. However, it is most questionable whether scoring by hand would be feasible except for a few cases. This table, and those preceding it, illustrate clearly how independence increases as the maximum weight increases.

T-SCORE FACTOR SCALES

Earlier in this chapter we discussed the factor scoring matrix which, when applied to the raw item score matrix, yields standardized mutually orthogonal factor scores. We also discussed integer response-weight scoring matrices where the integers are applied to the binary response element scores to yield factor scores. In this section, we consider a scoring matrix which, when applied to the raw score matrix, yields factor score distributions for the sample with means of about 50 and standard deviations of about 10. These values are not satisfied exactly because of rounding error. However, the factor scores have essentially zero correlations in the sample. We shall consider the T-score scoring matrix, the T-score factor score statistics, and the T-score correlation matrices for the two administrations.

T-SCORE SCORING MATRIX

Table 17 gives the first twenty rows and first ten columns of the 288 by 17 matrix of weights to be applied to the raw item scores (1 through 5) to give the seventeen sets of uncorrelated factor scores with means of about 50 and standard deviations of about 10. The last row of Table 17 is the vector of constants that are applied to a dummy vector with which the data matrix is augmented. This scoring procedure is not feasible with desk calculators. The availability of a computer equivalent to the IBM 709 or better is assumed.

T-SCORE FACTOR SCORE STATISTICS

Table 18 gives the T-score distributions for the ten factor scores in class intervals of 5 from 5 or less to 100 or more. For the most part, these are fairly normal. They tend to be slightly leptokurtic. The two rows at the bottom give the means and standard deviations, respectively, rounded to the nearest whole number.

Table 19 gives the intercorrelations of the first ten T-scores on the 422 observations, that is, the first and second administrations combined. Theoretically, these correlations should all be zero. Because of the approximation procedures in the principal axis solution and the rounding of the values in the scoring matrix, they are not precisely zero in the sample. If rounded to one decimal, however, most of them would be zero.

T-SCORE CORRELATIONS FOR BOTH ADMINISTRATIONS

If the 422-row data matrix is divided into first and second

Table 14. Factor Score Correlations, Maximum 3

First Administration

1	2	3	4	5	6	7	8	9	10
1.0	0.2	0.0	0.1	0.0	—0.1	0.0	0.1	0.1	0.1
0.2	1.0	0.2	0.2	0.2	0.2	0.2	0.2	0.1	—0.1
0.0	0.2	1.0	0.2	0.1	0.2	0.3	0.1	0.1	0.1
0.1	0.2	0.2	1.0	0.1	0.0	0.2	0.1	0.2	0.1
0.0	0.2	0.1	0.1	1.0	0.0	—0.1	0.0	0.0	—0.1
—0.1	0.2	0.2	0.0	0.0	1.0	0.1	0.0	0.1	—0.1
0.0	0.2	0.3	0.2	—0.1	0.1	1.0	0.1	—0.0	—0.1
0.1	0.2	0.1	0.1	0.0	0.0	0.1	1.0	0.0	0.2
0.1	0.1	0.1	0.2	0.0	0.1	—0.0	0.0	1.0	0.1
0.1	—0.1	0.1	0.1	—0.1	—0.1	0.1	0.2	0.1	1.0

First Administration with Second Administration

1	2	3	4	5	6	7	8	9	10
0.9	0.1	—0.0	0.1	0.1	—0.0	0.1	0.0	0.1	0.1
0.2	0.9	0.1	0.2	0.2	0.2	0.2	0.2	0.2	—0.1
—0.0	0.2	0.8	0.2	0.2	0.3	0.3	0.1	0.2	0.1
0.1	0.1	0.1	0.8	0.1	0.1	0.2	0.1	0.1	0.1

212

Second Administration

0.0	0.0	0.1	—0.1	0.0	0.7	0.1	0.1	0.2	—0.0
—0.1	0.0	0.0	0.1	0.8	0.1	0.1	0.1	0.1	0.1
0.0	0.1	0.1	0.8	0.2	0.0	0.1	0.3	0.3	0.1
0.1	0.1	0.7	0.1	0.0	0.0	0.1	0.0	0.1	0.1
0.0	0.8	0.0	—0.0	0.1	0.0	0.2	0.1	0.1	0.1
0.8	0.0	0.1	0.1	—0.1	—0.0	0.1	0.1	—0.1	0.1

0.1	0.1	0.1	0.1	0.1	0.1	0.1	0.0	0.2	1.0
—0.1	0.2	0.2	0.3	0.2	0.2	0.2	0.2	1.0	0.2
0.1	0.2	0.1	0.3	0.3	0.3	0.1	1.0	0.2	0.0
0.0	0.1	0.1	0.1	0.1	0.1	1.0	0.1	0.2	0.1
0.1	0.1	0.2	0.1	0.2	1.0	0.1	0.3	0.2	0.1
—0.1	0.1	0.1	0.2	1.0	0.2	0.1	0.3	0.2	0.1
0.1	0.1	0.1	1.0	0.1	0.1	0.1	0.3	0.3	0.1
0.1	0.1	1.0	0.1	0.2	0.2	0.1	0.1	0.2	0.1
—0.0	1.0	0.1	0.1	0.1	0.1	0.1	0.2	0.2	0.1
1.0	—0.0	0.0	0.1	0.1	—0.1	0.0	0.1	—0.1	0.1

Table 15. Factor Score Correlations, Maximum 5

First Administration

	1	2	3	4	5	6	7	8	9	10
	1.0	0.0	-0.0	-0.0	0.1	-0.2	-0.0	0.0	-0.1	-0.1
	0.0	1.0	0.1	-0.0	0.0	-0.1	0.0	0.1	0.0	0.0
	-0.0	0.1	1.0	0.1	0.1	-0.1	0.1	0.1	-0.0	0.2
	-0.0	-0.0	0.1	1.0	0.1	-0.0	0.1	0.1	0.0	0.0
	0.1	0.0	0.1	0.1	1.0	-0.1	-0.0	0.0	-0.0	-0.2
	-0.2	-0.1	-0.1	-0.0	-0.1	1.0	-0.0	0.0	-0.1	0.1
	-0.0	0.0	0.1	0.1	-0.0	-0.0	1.0	0.2	-0.1	0.1
	0.0	0.1	0.1	0.1	0.0	0.0	0.2	1.0	0.1	0.1
	-0.1	0.0	-0.0	0.0	-0.0	-0.1	-0.1	0.1	1.0	-0.0
	-0.1	0.0	0.2	0.0	-0.2	0.1	0.1	0.1	-0.0	1.0

First Administration with Second Administration

	1	2	3	4	5	6	7	8	9	10
	0.9	-0.0	-0.1	-0.0	0.1	-0.2	-0.0	-0.0	-0.1	-0.1
	0.0	0.9	0.0	-0.0	0.0	-0.1	0.1	0.0	0.0	-0.0
	-0.1	0.1	0.8	0.1	0.0	-0.1	0.1	0.0	0.0	0.1
	-0.0	0.0	0.1	0.8	-0.0	-0.1	0.1	0.2	0.0	-0.0

First Administration

—0.1	—0.0	0.1	0.0	—0.0	0.8	0.1	0.1	0.0	0.1
0.0	—0.1	—0.1	—0.1	0.8	0.0	—0.1	—0.0	—0.0	—0.1
—0.0	—0.1	0.2	0.8	—0.0	—0.0	0.0	0.1	0.1	0.0
0.0	0.1	0.8	0.1	0.0	—0.0	0.0	—0.0	0.0	0.1
—0.0	0.8	0.0	—0.2	—0.0	—0.0	—0.0	—0.0	0.1	—0.1
0.8	—0.1	0.0	0.0	0.0	—0.1	—0.0	0.1	—0.0	—0.1

Second Administration

—0.1	—0.1	—0.0	—0.0	—0.1	0.1	—0.0	—0.1	0.0	1.0
—0.1	0.0	0.0	0.1	—0.0	—0.0	—0.0	0.0	1.0	0.0
0.2	0.0	0.1	0.0	—0.1	0.1	0.1	1.0	0.0	—0.1
—0.1	—0.0	0.1	0.1	—0.1	—0.0	1.0	0.1	—0.0	—0.0
—0.1	0.0	0.0	—0.0	0.0	1.0	—0.0	0.1	—0.0	0.1
—0.0	—0.1	—0.0	—0.0	1.0	0.0	—0.1	—0.1	0.1	—0.1
0.0	—0.2	0.2	1.0	—0.0	—0.0	0.1	0.0	0.0	—0.0
0.0	0.0	1.0	0.2	—0.0	0.0	0.1	0.1	0.0	—0.1
—0.1	1.0	0.0	—0.2	—0.1	0.0	—0.0	0.0	—0.1	—0.1
1.0	—0.1	0.0	0.0	—0.0	—0.1	—0.1	0.2	—0.1	

215

Table 16. Factor Score Correlations, Maximum 9

First Administration

1	2	3	4	5	6	7	8	9	10
1.0	—0.0	—0.0	—0.1	—0.1	—0.0	—0.1	0.1	—0.0	0.1
—0.0	1.0	—0.0	—0.1	0.0	0.0	0.0	—0.0	—0.1	0.0
—0.0	—0.0	1.0	0.1	0.1	0.0	0.1	0.0	—0.0	0.0
—0.1	—0.1	0.1	1.0	0.0	0.0	0.0	0.1	0.0	0.0
—0.1	0.0	0.1	0.0	1.0	0.0	—0.0	—0.0	—0.0	—0.1
—0.0	0.0	0.0	0.0	0.0	1.0	—0.1	0.0	0.0	0.0
—0.1	0.0	0.1	0.0	—0.0	—0.1	1.0	0.0	—0.1	0.1
0.1	—0.0	0.0	0.1	—0.0	0.0	0.0	1.0	0.0	0.1
—0.0	—0.1	—0.0	0.0	—0.0	0.0	—0.1	0.0	1.0	0.0
0.1	0.0	0.0	0.0	—0.1	0.0	0.1	0.1	0.0	1.0

First Administration with Second Administration

1	2	3	4	5	6	7	8	9	10
0.9	—0.1	—0.0	—0.0	—0.0	0.1	—0.0	0.0	—0.0	0.0
—0.0	0.9	0.0	—0.0	0.0	0.0	—0.0	0.1	—0.1	0.0
—0.1	—0.0	0.9	0.0	0.1	0.0	0.0	—0.0	0.0	0.0
—0.1	—0.0	0.0	0.8	—0.0	0.0	0.0	0.0	—0.0	0.0

Second Administration

0.0	-0.1	0.0	0.0	0.0	0.8	0.0	0.1	0.0	-0.1
0.0	-0.0	-0.1	-0.1	0.8	0.1	0.1	0.1	0.0	0.0
0.0	-0.1	0.1	0.8	-0.0	-0.0	-0.1	0.1	0.0	0.0
0.1	0.0	0.8	0.1	0.0	-0.1	0.0	-0.0	0.0	0.1
-0.0	0.8	0.0	-0.1	-0.0	0.0	0.0	-0.0	-0.1	-0.0
0.9	0.0	0.1	0.1	-0.0	0.0	0.0	0.0	-0.0	0.1

0.0	-0.1	-0.0	0.0	0.1	-0.1	0.0	0.0	0.0	1.0
-0.0	-0.1	0.0	0.1	0.1	0.0	0.0	-0.1	1.0	-0.0
0.1	-0.1	-0.0	-0.0	0.0	0.1	-0.0	1.0	-0.1	0.0
0.0	-0.0	0.0	0.0	0.1	-0.1	1.0	-0.0	0.0	0.0
0.0	-0.0	-0.0	-0.0	0.1	1.0	-0.1	0.1	0.1	-0.1
-0.1	-0.1	0.1	1.0	1.0	0.1	0.1	0.0	0.1	0.1
0.0	-0.0	1.0	0.1	-0.0	-0.0	0.0	-0.0	0.0	0.0
0.1	1.0	-0.0	0.0	-0.0	-0.0	-0.0	-0.1	-0.1	-0.0
1.0	-0.1	0.0	0.0	0.0	0.0	0.0	0.1	-0.0	0.0

Table 17. T-Score Scoring Matrix

	1	2	3	4	5	6	7	8	9	10
1	—54	—15	—51	34	5	146	19	43	50	7
2	7	63	—27	—30	—47	53	—18	—15	35	—67
3	54	—17	8	—2	6	—31	—1	18	—1	1
4	—14	—0	—22	—33	—15	10	50	—15	11	14
5	3	6	14	—18	—9	4	—12	21	—3	—21
6	24	—4	—2	—0	—6	—12	—42	4	60	6
7	1	—20	53	7	7	—6	2	—15	36	15
8	20	7	—2	—31	15	45	—10	—18	—0	27
9	—11	—18	—9	—5	—52	3	11	46	15	129
10	7	12	—35	—21	—32	—1	13	—5	—10	—5
11	11	—20	54	3	—17	—65	—8	22	—6	5
12	—9	—28	—4	13	3	6	—32	50	105	13
13	—25	—12	23	15	12	3	35	9	—15	46
14	12	76	—10	—16	18	—2	—3	—17	—33	2
15	17	—2	—8	—7	20	12	18	62	0	14
16	—9	10	—4	—7	—52	23	10	—14	21	—16
17	—8	—18	1	—24	39	22	9	41	—40	26
18	29	—14	6	52	28	52	6	—57	—13	—5
19	21	4	10	—31	2	—3	—29	—32	—23	84
20	—11	14	—7	—46	—1	—15	11	24	25	—7
	42	—10	28	138	12	—66	26	95	28	24

Table 18. *T*-Score Distributions for Factor Scores

	1	2	3	4	5	6	7	8	9	10
1	1	0	0	1	1	2	0	0	0	0
2	1	1	0	1	1	0	1	1	2	1
3	0	0	0	0	3	1	1	0	1	1
4	1	0	2	4	4	4	2	0	0	2
5	3	2	2	2	2	2	2	2	0	5
6	6	4	2	5	8	5	10	7	4	4
7	8	17	13	11	16	9	14	20	14	25
8	37	32	47	39	25	36	32	28	57	28
9	68	86	87	81	61	56	65	72	61	72
10	85	95	85	88	81	110	93	88	92	78
11	90	55	72	63	110	95	95	92	100	80
12	60	69	45	61	60	49	59	51	31	69
13	35	32	35	44	31	27	22	35	27	31
14	16	18	17	16	12	17	11	14	17	20
15	5	6	8	4	4	5	10	7	11	5
16	3	2	2	2	3	1	3	4	2	1
17	2	2	3	0	0	2	0	0	2	0
18	0	1	2	0	0	0	0	0	1	0
19	1	0	0	0	0	1	2	0	0	0
20	0	0	0	0	0	0	0	1	0	0
	51.	50.	50.	50.	50.	50.	50.	50.	50.	50.
	10.	10.	10.	10.	11.	10.	10.	10.	10.	10.

Table 19. T-Score Intercorrelations of Factor Scores for Both Administrations

1.00	—0.00	0.01	0.01	—0.00	0.01	—0.02	—0.01	—0.01	0.00
—0.00	1.00	—0.02	—0.03	0.00	0.01	0.02	0.01	—0.02	—0.03
0.01	—0.02	1.00	0.00	0.01	—0.01	—0.00	0.00	—0.02	0.02
0.01	—0.03	0.00	1.00	—0.01	0.00	0.00	0.01	—0.01	0.01
—0.00	0.00	0.01	—0.01	1.00	0.00	—0.01	—0.02	—0.01	—0.03
0.01	0.01	—0.01	0.00	0.00	1.00	—0.02	—0.04	0.00	—0.01
—0.02	0.02	—0.00	0.00	—0.01	—0.02	1.00	0.03	—0.05	0.03
—0.01	0.01	0.00	0.01	—0.02	—0.04	0.03	1.00	—0.02	0.02
—0.01	—0.02	—0.02	—0.01	—0.01	0.00	—0.05	—0.02	1.00	—0.02
0.00	—0.03	0.02	0.01	—0.03	—0.01	0.03	0.02	—0.02	1.00

administration matrices, we can get the correlations among the *T*-factor scores for the first administration, for the first with the second, and for the second administration. These correlation sub-matrices for the first ten factors are given respectively in the three sections of Table 20. It will be noted that with very few exceptions the off-diagonal elements in all three sections do not exceed .1, and 539 or about two-thirds of them are .0 to the first decimal. The diagonal elements of the middle section are, of course, the retest reliabilities and none is less than .8.

Table 20. *T*-Score Correlation Submatrices for First and Second Administrations

First Administration

1	2	3	4	5	6	7	8	9	10
1.0	—0.0	—0.0	—0.0	0.0	—0.1	—0.1	0.0	—0.0	—0.0
—0.0	1.0	—0.0	—0.1	0.0	—0.0	—0.0	0.0	—0.0	—0.0
—0.0	—0.0	1.0	0.0	0.0	—0.0	0.0	0.0	0.0	0.0
—0.0	—0.1	0.0	1.0	0.0	—0.0	—0.0	0.1	0.0	0.0
0.0	0.0	0.0	0.0	1.0	—0.0	—0.0	—0.0	—0.0	—0.1
—0.1	—0.0	—0.0	—0.0	—0.0	1.0	—0.1	0.0	0.0	0.0
—0.1	—0.0	0.0	—0.0	—0.0	—0.1	1.0	0.0	—0.1	0.0
0.0	0.0	0.0	0.1	—0.0	0.0	0.0	1.0	—0.0	0.1
—0.0	—0.0	0.0	0.0	—0.0	0.0	—0.1	—0.0	1.0	0.0
—0.0	—0.0	0.0	0.0	—0.1	0.0	0.0	0.1	0.0	1.0

First Administration with Second Administration

1	2	3	4	5	6	7	8	9	10
0.9	—0.1	—0.0	—0.0	0.1	—0.0	—0.0	—0.0	0.0	0.0
—0.0	0.9	0.0	—0.0	0.0	—0.0	—0.1	0.1	—0.0	0.0
—0.0	—0.0	0.9	0.0	0.0	—0.0	0.0	—0.0	0.1	0.0
—0.0	—0.0	—0.0	0.8	—0.0	—0.0	0.0	0.0	—0.0	0.0

—0.0	0.0	0.0	0.0	0.9	—0.0	0.0	0.0	—0.1	0.0
0.0	—0.0	0.0	0.0	0.1	0.8	—0.1	—0.1	—0.0	0.0
—0.0	0.0	0.1	—0.1	—0.0	—0.0	0.8	0.1	—0.1	—0.1
0.0	0.0	—0.0	—0.0	—0.0	0.0	0.0	0.8	0.0	0.0
—0.0	—0.0	0.0	0.0	0.0	—0.0	—0.1	0.0	0.9	—0.0
0.0	—0.0	0.0	0.0	0.0	—0.0	0.0	0.1	—0.0	0.9

Second Administration

1.0	—0.0	0.0	0.0	0.0	0.1	0.0	—0.0	0.0	0.0
—0.0	1.0	—0.1	0.0	—0.0	0.0	0.1	0.0	—0.0	—0.0
0.0	—0.1	1.0	—0.0	0.0	—0.0	—0.0	—0.0	—0.0	0.0
0.0	0.0	—0.0	1.0	—0.0	0.0	0.0	—0.0	—0.0	0.0
0.0	—0.0	0.0	—0.0	1.0	0.0	—0.0	—0.0	—0.0	0.0
0.1	0.0	—0.0	0.0	0.0	1.0	0.0	—0.1	—0.0	—0.1
0.0	0.1	—0.0	0.0	—0.0	0.0	1.0	0.0	—0.1	0.0
—0.0	0.0	—0.0	—0.0	—0.0	—0.1	0.0	1.0	—0.0	—0.0
0.0	—0.0	—0.0	—0.0	—0.0	—0.0	—0.1	—0.0	1.0	—0.1
0.0	—0.0	0.0	0.0	0.0	—0.1	0.0	—0.0	—0.1	1.0

Bibliography

ADLER, A. *Practice and Theory of Individual Psychology.* New York: Harcourt, 1927.

BELL, H. M. *The Adjustment Inventory: Manual for Student Form,* 1934; *Manual for Adult Form,* 1938. Stanford: Stanford University Press.

BERNREUTER, R. G. *The Personality Inventory: Manual.* Stanford: Stanford University Press, 1935.

BINET, A., and SIMON, T. "Méthodes Nouvelles pour le Diagnostic du Niveau Intellectuel des Anormaux," *Année Psychologique,* 1905, *11,* 191–244.

BLOOM, B. S. *Taxonomy of Educational Objectives, Handbook I: Cognitive Domain.* New York: Longmans, 1956.

BLOXOM, B. M. "Anger-Arousing Instructions and the Simplex in a Personality Questionnaire." Unpublished doctoral dissertation, University of Washington, 1966.

BROGDEN, H. E. "An Approach to the Problem of Differential Classification," *Psychometrika,* 1946, *11,* 139–154.

BURKET, G. R. "A Study of Reduced Rank Models for Multiple Prediction," *Psychometric Monographs,* No. 12, 1964.

CAMPBELL, M. M. "The Primary Dimensions of Item Ratings on Scales Designed to Measure Twenty-four of Murray's Manifest Needs." Unpublished doctoral dissertation, University of Washington, 1959.

CARROLL, J. B. "The Nature of Data, or How to Choose a Correlation Coefficient," *Psychometrika,* 1961, *26,* 347–372.

CATTELL, R. B. *Factor Analysis.* New York: Harper, 1952.

CATTELL, R. B. *Personality and Motivation: Structure and Measurement.* New York: Harcourt, Brace, 1957.

CLEMANS, W. V. "An Analytical and Empirical Examination of Some Properties of Ipsative Measures," *Psychometric Monographs,* No. 14, 1966.

DWYER, P. S. "Solution of the Personnel Classification Problem With the Method of Optimal Regions," *Psychometrika,* 1954, *19,* 11–26.

EDWARDS, A. L. *Edwards Personal Preference Schedule.* New York: Psychological Corporation, 1953.

EDWARDS, A. L. *The Social Desirability Variable in Personality Research.* New York: Dryden Press, 1957.

EDWARDS, A. L. "Social Desirability and Performance on the MMPI," *Psychometrika,* 1964, *29,* 295–308.

FLANAGAN, J. C. Unpublished notes, 1949.

FLANAGAN, J. C. "The Critical Incidents Technique," *Psychological Bulletin,* 1954, *51,* 327–358.

FREUD, S. *The Basic Writings of Sigmund Freud* (A. A. Brill, ed.). New York: Random House, 1938.

GUILFORD, J. P. *Personality.* New York: McGraw-Hill, 1959.

GUTTMAN, L. In P. Horst et al., *Prediction of Personal Adjustment,* Social Science Research Bulletin 48, 1941.

GUTTMAN, L. "The Determinacy of Factor Score Matrices with Implications for Five Other Basic Problems of Common-Factor Theory," *British Journal of Statistical Psychology,* 1955, *8,* 65–81.

GUTTMAN, L. "To What Extent Can Communalities Reduce Rank?", *Psychometrika,* 1958, *23,* 297–308.

HARMON, H. H. *Modern Factor Analysis.* Chicago: University of Chicago Press, 1967.

HASE, H. D., and GOLDBERG, L. R. "The Comparative Validity of Different Strategies of Deriving Personality Inventory Scales." Unpublished manuscript, 1966.

HATHAWAY, S. R., and MEEHL, P. E. *An Atlas for the Clinical Use of the MMPI.* Minneapolis: University of Minnesota Press, 1951.

HOLZINGER, K. J., and HARMON, H. H. *Factor Analysis.* Chicago: University of Chicago Press, 1941.

HORST, P. *The Prediction of Personal Adjustment.* Social Science Research Bulletin 48, 1941.

HORST, P. "A Technique for the Development of a Differential Prediction Battery," *Psychological Monographs,* No. 380, 1954.

HORST, P. "A Technique for the Development of a Multiple Absolute Prediction Battery," *Psychological Monographs,* No. 390, 1955.

HORST, P. "Optimal Estimates of Multiple Criteria with Restriction on the Covariance Matrix of Estimated Criteria," *Psychological Reports,* Monograph Supplement 6-V6, 1960.

HORST, P. "The Logic of Personnel Selection and Classification." In R. M. Gagné, et al., *Psychological Principles in System Development.* New York: Holt, 1962, pp. 231–271.

HORST, P. *Matrix Algebra for Social Scientists.* New York: Holt, 1963.

HORST, P. "Matrix Factoring and Test Theory." In N. Frederiksen and H. Gulliksen (Eds.), *Contributions to Mathematical Psychology.* New York: Holt, 1964a, pp. 129–140.

HORST, P. "Pattern Analysis and Configural Scoring," *Journal of Clinical Psychology,* 1964b, *10.*

HORST, P. *Factor Analysis of Data Matrices.* New York: Holt, 1965.

HORST, P. *Psychological Measurement and Prediction.* Belmont, Calif.: Wadsworth, 1966.

HOTELLING, H. "Analysis of a Complex of Statistical Variables into Principal Components," *Journal of Educational Psychology,* 1933, *24,* 417–441, 498–520.

JACKSON, D. N., and MESSICK, S. "Content and Style in Personality Assessment," *Psychological Bulletin,* 1958, *55,* 243–252.

JOHNSON, R. M. "Re-Analysis of Mosier's Factor Analysis of Neurotic Items." Unpublished master's dissertation, University of Washington, 1957.

JUNG, C. G. *Psychological Types.* New York: Harcourt, 1933.

KAISER, H. F. "The Varimax Criterion for Analytic Rotation in Factor Analysis," *Psychometrika,* 1958, *23,* 187–200.

KARR, C. "A Comparison of EPPS Scores Obtained from the Standard

Forced-Choice Procedure and a Rating Scale Format." Unpub-lished doctoral dissertation, University of Washington, 1958.

KELLEY, T. L. "Essential Traits of Mental Life," *Harvard Studies in Education*, 26. Cambridge: Harvard University Press, 1935.

KUDER, G. F. *Preference Record*. Chicago: University of Chicago Press, 1939.

KUDER, G. F., and RICHARDSON, M. W. "The Theory of the Estimation of Test Reliability," *Psychometrika*, 1937, 2, 151–160.

LEIMAN, J. M. "The Calculation of Regression Weights from Common Factor Loadings." Unpublished doctoral dissertation, University of Washington, 1951.

LORD, F. M. "Notes on a Problem of Multiple Classification," *Psychometrika*, 1952, 17, 3.

MCDONALD, R. P. "Nonlinear Factor Analysis," *Psychometric Monographs*, No. 15, 1967.

MCNEMAR, Q. "Lost: Our Intelligence? Why?" *American Psychologist*, 1964, 19, 871–882.

MCQUITTY, L. L. "Agreement Analysis: Classifying Persons by Predominant Patterns of Responses," *British Journal of Statistical Psychology*, 1956, *IX*, Part I, 17–20.

MEEHL, P. E. "Configural Scoring," *Journal of Consulting Psychology*, 1950, 14, 165–171.

MEREDITH, W. "On Appropriate Misuses of the Correlation Coefficient." Unpublished manuscript, 1964.

MURRAY, H. A., et al. *Explorations in Personality*. New York: Oxford University Press, 1938.

OSBURN, H. G., and LUBIN, A. "The Use of Configural Analysis for the Evaluation of Test Scoring Methods," *Psychometrika*, 1957, 22, 359–372.

RICHARDSON, M. W. Personal communication, 1933.

ROUDABUSH, G. E. "A Study in Prediction from Biographical Information." Unpublished doctoral dissertation, University of Washington, 1963.

RUCH, G. M. *The Objective or New Type Examination*. Chicago: Scott, Foresman, 1929.

RUNDQUIST, E. A., and SLETTO, R. F. *Personality in the Depression*. Minneapolis: University of Minnesota Press, 1936.

SARASON, I. G. *Personality: An Objective Approach*. New York: Wiley, 1966.

SCHMID, J., and LEIMAN, J. M. "The Development of Hierarchical Factor Solutions," *Psychometrika*, 1957, *22*, 53–61.

SORENSON, R. C. "Development and Evaluation of a Matrix Transformation Useful in Personnel Classification." Unpublished doctoral dissertation, University of Washington, 1965.

SPEARMAN, C. *The Abilities of Man.* New York: Macmillan, 1927.

STENQUIST, J. L. *Stenquist Mechanical Aptitude Tests: Manual.* Yonkers-on-Hudson, N.Y.: World, 1922.

STRONG, JR., E. K. *Vocational Interests of Men and Women.* Stanford: Stanford University Press, 1943.

TERMAN, L. M. *The Measurement of Intelligence.* Boston: Houghton Mifflin, 1916.

TERMAN, L. M., and MERRILL, M. A. *Measuring Intelligence.* Boston: Houghton Mifflin, 1937.

THORNDIKE, E. L., et al. *The Measurement of Intelligence.* New York: Teachers College, Columbia University, Bureau of Publications, 1927.

THORNDIKE, R. L. "The Problem of Classification of Personnel," *Psychometrika*, 1950, *15*, 215–235.

THURSTONE, L. L. "Primary Mental Abilities," *Psychometric Monographs*, No. 1, 1938.

THURSTONE, L. L. *Multiple Factor Analysis.* Chicago: University of Chicago Press, 1947.

THURSTONE, L. L., and CHAVE, E. J. *The Measurement of Attitude.* Chicago: University of Chicago Press, 1929.

THURSTONE, L. L., and THURSTONE, T. G. "Factorial Studies of Intelligence," *Psychometric Monographs*, No. 2, 1941.

TRYON, R. C. "Cluster or Factor Analysis of Variables or Persons Unrestricted by Their Numbers," *American Psychologist*, 1965, *20*, 545.

TUCKER, L. R. "An Inter-Battery Method of Factor Analysis," *Psychometrika*, 1958, *23*, 111–136.

TUCKER, L. R. "Implications of Factor Analysis of Three-Way Matrices for Measurement of Change." In C. W. Harris (Ed.), *Problems in Measuring Change.* Madison: University of Wisconsin Press, 1963, pp. 122–137.

VOTAW, JR., D. F. "Methods of Solving Some Personnel Classification Problems," *Psychometrika*, 1952, *17*, 3.

WAINWRIGHT, G. E. "Configural Analysis." Unpublished doctoral dissertation, University of Washington, 1965.

WRIGHT, C. E. "Relations Between Normative and Ipsative Measures of Personality." Unpublished doctoral dissertation, University of Washington, 1957.

Index

A

Achievement tests, 13–14, 26
Acquiescence, 50, 52
Adjustment: inventories, 23; personal, 23
ADLER, A., 51
Answer: best, 37, 38; correct, 14, 17, 49, 51; keyed, 49; right, 37
Answer sheets, 7–8, 28–29, 30; multiple choice, 11; scoring of, 99
Approximation: to correlation matrix, 106, 157; to data matrix, 90, 104; least square, 106; to normalize data matrix, 108; reduced rank data matrix, 127–128, 165; to three-mode data matrix, 153
Aptitude tests, 12

Attitude: measurement inventory, 24; scores, 117
Attribute mode, and scaling theory, 153
Attribute-occasion by entity matrix, 151
Attributes, 44–47, 73–74, 150, 151, 152, 153; in categorical sets, 128; by entity-occasions, 150–151; and origin, 130; scaling of, 123, 152

B

Basic structure solution, 152, 167
Behavior statements, 74
BELL, H. M., 23, 47
BERNREUTER, R. G., 47
Binary data matrix, 18, 19, 129; cri-

Index